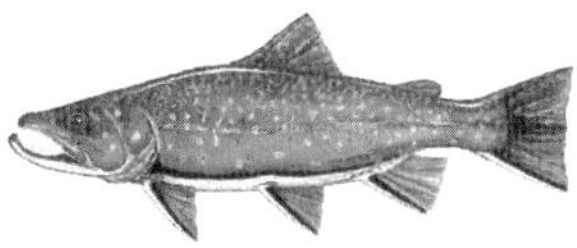

True Stories of Maine Fly Fishermen

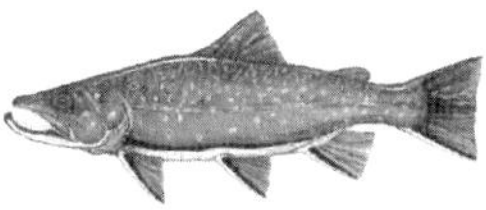

J.H. Hall

THE History PRESS

Published by The History Press
Charleston, SC 29403
www.historypress.net

Cover image: Dan Onion on the upper Kennebago River.
All images courtesy of the author.

"Scales," "My Time Among the Mainers" and "Fishing Partners" were in *Selling Fish* © Stackpole Books 2000. "The Value of Flies," "Guiding the Guide," "To Nymph or Not to Nymph," "The Margaree, the Miramichi and Irving," "Wally" and "Reading Proust in Montana" first appeared in *Flyfishing & Tying Journal*. "Bright Fish, Nice City" originally appeared in *City Fishing* © Stackpole Books 2002. "Pollock Rock" was first published in *Salt Water Sportsman*.

First published 2008

Manufactured in the United States

ISBN 978.1.59629.460.8

Library of Congress Cataloging-in-Publication Data
Hall, J. H.
True stories of Maine fly fishermen / J.H. Hall.
p. cm.
ISBN 978-1-59629-460-8
1. Fly fishing--Maine--Anecdotes. 2. Fishers--Maine--Anecdotes. I. Title.
SH503.H35 2008
799.12'409741--dc22
2007052355

Notice: The information in this book is true and complete to the best of our knowledge. It is offered without guarantee on the part of the author or The History Press. The author and The History Press disclaim all liability in connection with the use of this book.

For Preston and Evan

Contents

Scales

"I must be the worst fisherman who ever wet a line," I told myself after yet another conversation with yet another fly fisherman whose fish were consistently larger than mine. That was in the late 1970s, and I was new to fly-fishing. No doubt in time I, too, would learn to catch the larger fish.

Time passed, but the pattern did not change; if anything, the gap widened. Where I caught two-pound bass, others caught fish of three, four, sometimes even five pounds. Where I caught fourteen-inch trout, theirs were sixteen, seventeen, sometimes eighteen. My sixteen-inch landlocked salmon were dwarfed by theirs of twenty-plus inches. My fishing skills, instead of improving, were evidently deteriorating.

Then one summer morning on David Pond in central Maine, an excited fifteen-year-old boy came running over from the next cabin holding a nice smallmouth bass he'd caught while fishing with his father. He knew the fish weighed three pounds, because his father said it did, but he wanted to see if it might weigh even more. I measured the fish at fifteen inches, not much belly.

"That's a nice fish," I said, "but it won't go three pounds." I knew this because I actually weighed my fish on accurate scales, an old habit I'd acquired during a brief stint fishing commercially on the Chesapeake, where finfish are sold by weight, and crabs by length (and gender).

The boy, knowing nothing of this, caring nothing, knew better. "It's at least three," he insisted.

Reluctantly I weighed the fish: 1.5 pounds.

"There's something wrong with those scales," he said.

"Look," I said, "that's a nice fish, no matter what it weighs, but a smallmouth usually won't top three pounds until it's over seventeen inches, sometimes not even then."

The kid wasn't buying it. That was a three-pound fish because his father said it was, and his father had seen another fish that same morning that would've weighed seven pounds! His faith in his father and his love of fishing were so touching that I did not bother arguing, but I did become, belatedly, a bit skeptical of other people's catches.

After that episode, whenever someone boasted of fish size, I would ask what sort of scales they weighed them on. I would use the same tone of voice I used to inquire about fly selection or line weight: I was curious, just trying to learn; by no means was I challenging their veracity. Invariably the response would be, "I didn't actually weigh him, but when you've caught enough, you can just tell."

"Oh."

So there, I realized after a few such conversations, was my answer: other people caught larger fish than I did because they never measured them. Maybe I shouldn't have measured them either.

I once had a guide tell me, "Measuring a fish insults the fish," and his point is well taken. Size alone is by no means the true measure of the fish. Too many other factors come into play, such as setting, size of water in which the fish was caught, the fight and so on. But there is such a thing as science and, sadly for fishing romantics, science involves numbers.

In those days I kept a diary for Maine Inland Fisheries. At the end of every season I submitted my statistics: number of fish caught, size, species, location and fishing method. I took my responsibility seriously, since inaccurately optimistic measurements could have led the biologists into thinking that the fishery was healthier than it actually was. I owed it to the fish to relate the facts, same as a doctor owes it to his patient to record an accurate blood pressure, rather than what the doctor wishes it were. A doctor may not wish to bluntly tell his patient that he has terminal cancer and six months to live, but *somebody* needs to know.

So in that spirit, I continued to take a hard line on fish data, believing that I stood for truth, justice and a healthy fishery. Then along came Kirby.

On my son Evan's ninth birthday, a group of his friends came to our place on Lovejoy Pond. Serious, dark-haired, dark-eyed Kirby asked if I would take him fishing. Would I ever! If only my own sons had ever asked!

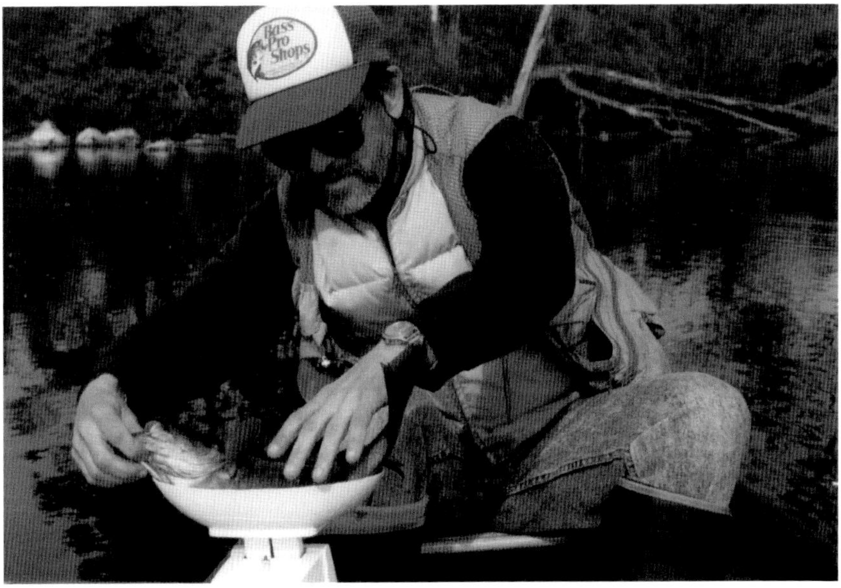

From the days when the author thought accurate fish weights were important.

I paddled the canoe while Kirby trolled a Mepp's spinner, occasionally casting to a dock or log. Soon he hooked a spunky largemouth near a partially sunken dock. The fish jumped—it was about ten inches, less than a pound—and then dove. Kirby reeled hard, perhaps too hard, and the next time the fish jumped, it threw the lure. We did not fish long and that was the only fish he hooked, but at least he hooked something, and there were no major accidents, no self-inflicted wounds and we hadn't capsized; I called it a win.

Just before we reached home, Kirby said, tentatively, "I'm going to say we *caught* that fish, OK?"

I said, "Kirby, you absolutely caught that fish. That's what we call a 'long-distance release.'"

"And," he added turning to face me, "I'm going to say it was about this big." He held his hands about fifteen inches apart.

"It was all of that," I said. "Maybe more."

I could hardly believe my ears. I was encouraging this child, who already had a reputation for exaggeration, to lie. But, of course, he understood that because of his reputation, if he told the truth, his friends would assume he was exaggerating and would mark his fish down to seven or eight inches, and that fish was much larger than any seven or eight inches. Therefore, in order to arrive at the truth, Kirby had to lie, and I had to help him. It was my responsibility same as it was my responsibility, for that day, to feed those boys and keep them safe.

Later I realized that this was probably how exaggerating fish size all began: it was transmitted from father, or surrogate father, to son or daughter, not out of a need to impress, but out of love. It's the same impulse that leads us to over-praise our children's efforts in school or sports. "Good job!" we yell at a child's most feeble, clumsy efforts on the soccer field. And not only is it not harmful, it is our duty as parents to tell these soothing lies. There's plenty of time later for them to learn life's cruel truths. Let somebody else teach those.

After that incident I tried to be more philosophical about fish size. Recently, though, on the Kennebago River, my philosophy was put to the test. The Kennebago is fabled water; a train once carried sports from Rangeley to camps on Kennebago Lake. That July Fourth the river was running high, good for landlocked salmon chasing smelts. Some of my usual spots weren't fishable, but others that were usually too shallow now held salmon. In the first pool I caught two sixteen-inch fish, not huge, but bright, fresh and feistier than fall-run fish. One fish still carried in the corner of its mouth a Black Ghost streamer, tied with real Jungle Cock, indicating a fly tied by a serious fisherman. It put my less well-tied Gray Ghost to shame, but then again, I had the fish in hand, *and* the other fly.

In the next pool I struck it rich. Standing on a rock in midstream, casting down and across a confusion of currents, I hooked fish after fish, including two eighteen-inchers, and lost another about that size. It almost never happens like that—midsummer, midday, sun bearing down—but the fish were insanely aggressive, chasing the fly, jumping wildly. I hooked over a dozen, and in the melee lost that Black Ghost and a nice landing net, but I was too frenzied and euphoric to care. I scrambled ashore, plowed back into the brush and headed downriver to where I'd started, anticipating, now that I'd rested that pool, another bonanza.

Instead, I found another fisherman. I almost never encounter anyone else at that pool. It is not remote—nothing on the Kennebago is remote—but it is tucked away, unmarked and unmapped. But there he sat on the tailgate of his pickup, pulling off his waders. He had the same dazed, euphoric look on his face that I no doubt had on mine, up until the moment I saw him.

The fisherman introduced himself—his name was Bill—and offered me a beer. I declined. "How'd you do?" I asked unnecessarily. He'd obviously done well.

"Fabulous!" he said. Between the previous evening and this morning, he'd caught four fish over twenty inches. At that time, I'd fished that river fifteen years, and never caught even one legitimate twenty-inch fish. Even now, some years later, I've measured but a single fish from that river over twenty inches.

"What'd you catch them on?" I asked.

"Streamers and weighted nymphs. They're holding right on the bottom."

"What streamers?"

He mentioned several familiar patterns, including the Black Ghost.

"I caught a fish this morning that had a Black Ghost stuck in the corner of its mouth."

He smiled and shook his head. "I broke off a cawker last night." "Cawker," meaning "corker," is local parlance for a really nice fish.

"I noticed the fly because it was so well-tied."

"Thanks."

"It looked like real Jungle Cock."

He smiled, sipped his beer and told me where he'd located a legal source of domestic Jungle Cock. No question, it was his fly all right, and his fish.

"That fish was twenty-two inches long," I said.

Bill was not the least bit fazed. "I knew he was a cawker."

I smiled; I had him now. "Nah, I'm just shittin' you. That fish was actually sixteen inches."

Bill didn't bat an eye. Sixteen inches, twenty-two—what difference did it make? A cawker was a cawker. If I wanted to play games, his demeanor implied, that was my problem. He was right, too.

I realized, finally, there are two types of numbers. One type we report to Inland Fisheries, and the other we use in conversation. They're as different as centimeters are from inches. In conversation, units of measure are figures of speech, metaphors. The answer to the question, "How big was that fish?" is "How big does it need to be to gain your respect?" Not your respect for my prowess as a fisherman, but for the fish. In the right hands, it's not bragging to exaggerate fish size, and I had to admit, Bill's seemed like the right hands. He wasn't boasting; he was just happy, same as I ought to have been if I had any sense.

"On second thought," I said, after a silence, "maybe I will have that beer. If the offer still stands."

It did. We sat on the tailgate, making small talk, counting our blessings—a beautiful day, gorgeous river full of aggressive fish, not much competition, light breeze and not *too* many black flies. Before long I was starting to feel pretty mellow myself. After all, it's not every day that I take three twenty-one-inch fish from a single pool.

Posted

I found the water in June of 1990, when my friend John Yindra and I drifted the St. George River below Searsmont, Maine. We floated through beautiful pools and runs, but did not see a fish until we reached an oxbow section above Appleton, where fish were rising, large fish to judge by their swirls. John tied the canoe to an overhanging alder, while I made futile casts with a dry.

"I think they're nymphing," John said.

"I think they are too." But while I was thinking and flailing away, John was tying on a nymph, and now it was his turn.

On his first cast with a pheasant tail, he hooked and broke off a good fish. He quickly retied, cast again and another nice fish took, and this time, eventually, he landed it, a two-and-a-half-pound brown, beautifully marked. There were no more rises and the canoe was leaking from an earlier encounter with a rock, so we called it a day—a successful day. We had found new water not far from home, and at least one of us had caught a fish. We agreed to try this again.

The trouble with canoe trips is that they usually take two people and two vehicles, and the Maine fishing season is short. Time and logistics kept us off the St. George until 1993, and that time we caught nothing. One trip every three years was not the way to learn a river.

Then John and I lost touch for a while, but neither of us forgot those nice browns. I didn't know many places near Augusta that offered such fish. It was only forty minutes from work. I studied maps and reconnoitered the property. The water was accessible from shore, but the adjacent land was posted. The signs were old, though, and maybe

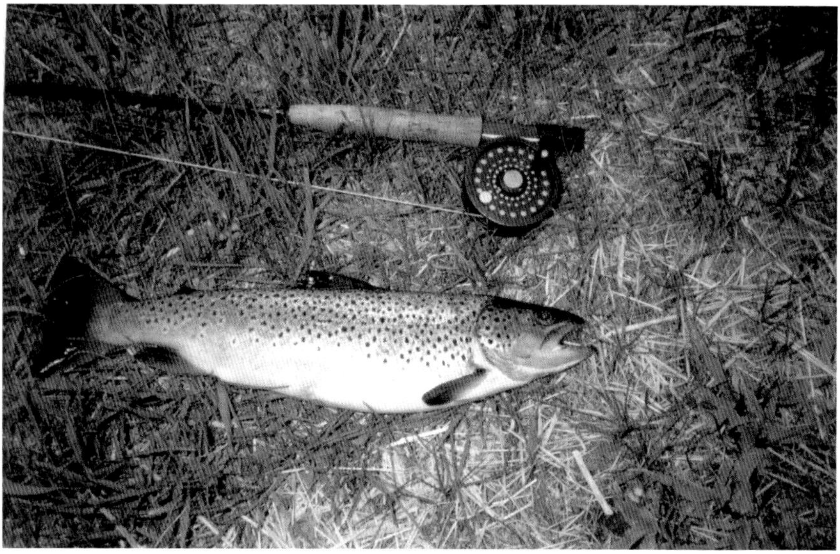

John Yindra's brown trout from the St. George River.

obsolete, no longer legally binding. Maybe. That good pool was virtually impossible to reach from the other side, which, anyhow, was also posted. That didn't leave many options.

One May afternoon in 1996, I walked up to the landowner's house wearing waders and carrying a fly rod, a uniform that I hoped would identify me as one of the "good guys," or, if not good, at least harmless. Everybody knows that fly fishermen do not litter or leave gates open. That's the other guys. I knocked on the door and a woman answered. She looked to be in her late fifties and not particularly happy to see a stranger at her house. I introduced myself. "I wanted to see about getting permission to fish the river from your property," I said.

"I'll get my husband," she said brusquely.

Soon her husband, Virgil, appeared. He was a rugged, middle-aged man, wearing soiled dungarees, a green flannel shirt and work shoes. He stepped outside, a good sign. The door could not be slammed in my face. We stood in his driveway; behind us was a lawn tractor, and behind that a big garden, then the meadow and river. I told him what I'd come for. His wife must have told him too, because he started shaking his head before I even finished my presentation.

"I don't let people fish from my property," he said firmly.

"Really? Why is that?"

"The state won't let me fish with worms. I don't let people on my place."

This was bad. I knew that section was fly-fishing only; that's why I wanted to fish it. But I didn't know the past history. Now my fly rod and waders made me the enemy.

Virgil looked wistfully back toward the meadow. "I used to take my little grandson down there and fish with worms. Used to be some nice trout in there. Brook trout, not these new ones. Now they say I can't do that. Got to fish with flies, and I don't cast. They won't let me plant that field back there either. It's wetlands or something. Can't even fertilize it."

"That doesn't seem fair," I said. "Seems like they ought to cut the adjacent landowners a little slack."

He nodded.

This was tough. Virgil's story reminded me of my ancestors on the Chesapeake, whose waterfowling was seriously crimped when the state imposed seasons and limits, and outlawed the use of bait. I told Virgil about those relatives, their resentment of the state and how their situation reminded me of his. Virgil was unmoved, as well he should have been. Some stranger knocks on your door and tells you his life story, and you're supposed see the light? No, Virgil had more integrity than that.

Next I offered to show him how to fly-cast. "It's not that hard. If I can do it, anybody can. Then you could teach your grandson, and wouldn't that be something?"

That just made things worse. He didn't say it, but I saw that Virgil's refusal to fly-fish wasn't due to lack of ability. It was a matter of principle. And here I came trying to compromise those principles and sell him a newfangled way of fishing. Even though I had the law on my side, I did not feel like the good guy; I felt like a traveling salesman. And Virgil was just standing up for what he believed in, same as my relatives, who somehow understood that it wasn't their hunting practices that harmed the duck population. There were larger forces at work, far away. The same forces that made the laws necessary made the laws.

So I quit trying to sell Virgil a "bill of goods," and I didn't preach to him about the virtues of fly-fishing, catch-and-release and brown trout. And maybe *because* I didn't, before he went back inside, Virgil granted me permission to fish.

"But just you," he said.

"Thank you *very* much," I said.

The next time down I left Virgil the book of stories I had written about my family on the Chesapeake. I wanted him to know that I hadn't just made that up for the moment; that I meant it. I quietly left the book inside the front door, because I did not wish to disturb Virgil and, frankly, I didn't want to risk seeing the wife again.

I didn't fish that stretch of the St. George very often, or catch many fish, and I never caught a large one like John's. But I liked going there from time to time, because it was nearby and private, my own little stretch of water, my personal brown trout laboratory. It was what I imagined fishing in England might be like, with flat water, weeds and casting only to rising fish.

Usually I would give Virgil a call the night before I planned to fish, just to touch base and let him know I'd be around. A couple of times I took another person, and cleared that too, but more often I fished alone. On one such spring evening, a young, pregnant woman meandered by the river. The edge of the meadow was easy walking, with a park-like charm. I reeled in and went over and chatted with her. I told her who I was and that I had Virgil's permission to fish. "Are you his daughter?" I asked.

"Daughter-in-law," she said. Then slightly embarrassed, she added, "Well, sort of. We're not actually…"

I waved her off. No need to explain. If she was good enough for Virgil, she was good enough for me. We talked a few more minutes and she continued her walk. If anything, her visit added to the pleasure of the evening and to the sense of privacy, almost intimacy: *nobody* had access to that water except family, "sort of" family and me. Maybe those Chesapeake stories had struck a chord in Virgil, after all. I never asked, didn't dare, but it's every writer's fantasy that someone will read and be moved by what he or she has written. Granted that many of those fantasies involve members of the opposite sex, there are worse things for a fly fisherman than to make meaningful contact with a farmer whose land lies adjacent a beautiful trout stream.

Then for a couple of years, I didn't fish the St. George at all. I had other places to fish, and I suppose I took the St. George for granted. I neglected my relationship with Virgil, and I paid for my neglect.

One spring not long ago, I had the urge to fish the St. George again. I missed the quiet evenings of rising fish, even if I usually couldn't catch the fish. So I gave Virgil a call. Unfortunately, his wife answered. "Could I speak to Virgil?" I said in my nicest possible voice.

"Who is this?"

I gave her my name, and told her that I was the fellow who Virgil had let fish from his property. "I just wanted to make sure it was still okay." She hung up.

I called back, hoping that maybe we just got cut off. No answer, and no answering machine.

I decided not to go that year.

But the next year, I reconsidered. I *still* wanted to fish that water. I was a better, more versatile fisherman now, and I had some unfinished business with those browns. But this time I wouldn't bother calling ahead. Virgil never said I had to; I just did it as a courtesy, and if my consideration wasn't going to be reciprocated, fine. The last time I talked to Virgil, I had permission to fish. His wife hadn't rescinded it; she just hung up. That could have meant anything. And who said she even represented Virgil? She might have hijacked my relationship with Virgil without telling him. If he knew how she treated *me*, the author of the stories that explained Virgil's own life to himself, he might have been furious. So, for the sake of all concerned, I didn't call. I just went.

I parked in the usual place, but instead of walking through the open meadow, I hugged the river, sometimes wading, sometimes in the alders. In those places where I couldn't avoid exposure, I looked first, moved fast and kept my head low. When I reached the oxbow section, I stayed beneath the horizon of bank. And I fished. I even caught a couple of small ones, but it wasn't the same. For one thing, there weren't many fish rising. Maybe the state had quit stocking because the stretch had no public access. But aside from that, it didn't feel the same. I felt unwelcome, and I did not like the feeling.

There are places where trespassing might actually *enhance* the fishing pleasure. Some waters that were accessible for decades and then fell into the unclean hands of newly minted multimillionaires—I'd trespass on those in a heartbeat. But Virgil was not a newly minted millionaire or newcomer. Virgil was a farmer and a Mainer; he was here first. That had to be respected, if not by the state of Maine, at least by me.

Later that summer I ran into John Yindra in the Wayne Post Office, and naturally we talked fishing. John had also recently tried to fish the St. George. He'd gone to the house and knocked on the door, but was denied access. "Virgil is still mad at the state," John said. "They won't let him fish with worms. So he's not letting anybody on."

I said, "I know, but I went anyway."

"You did?"

"Yeah, but I didn't stay long or catch much." I told him about the phone call the year before. "I don't think I'll be going back. I think it's time to leave Virgil in peace. He's suffered enough."

John seemed to think so too.

The Value of Flies

Once at a party I was discussing fly-fishing with an attractive woman, who informed me that her boyfriend, who was not at the party, had recently caught a trout on a fly that he had tied himself. "Isn't that about the ultimate?" she asked.

I said, "The 'ultimate' is really just catching a fish on a fly. It doesn't much matter where the fly came from. It's not about the fly or the fisherman. It's about the fish."

She wasn't buying it, or me, and she moved off.

So be it. I spoke the truth as it had been revealed to me in the summer of 1975 on the South Branch of the Dead River near Stratton, Maine, when I caught a nine-inch brook trout on the first fly that I had ever tied. Not on the first pattern that I had perfected, but on the actual inaugural effort itself, a very scraggly Warden's Worry, a bucktail, the perfect starting place for the novitiate. But catching that trout most certainly did not feel like the "ultimate." I wasn't proud of myself; I was embarrassed for the fish. I had read glowing reports of the brook trout, and now one had demeaned the whole species by mistaking my absurd conglomeration of chenille and fur for, of all things, food! What kind of fish *was* this? What kind of sport?

As it turned out, it was a wonderful sport, so wonderful it surpasses the term "sport," and the brook trout is a wonderful fish, even if one did take my first fly. That was probably a hatchery fish, and I've been humbled by enough wild brook trout since to have learned never to take any fish for granted.

I continued tying flies, but in 1980, when I discovered bass fishing, I started with store-bought poppers, Bass Dusters and Sneaky Petes. Then I decided that to be a "real" fly fisherman, I ought to tie my own bass flies too. So I did, but they all came out resembling deer hair versions of Bass Dusters and Sneaky Petes, upon which they were modeled, and I felt no greater thrill catching bass on my flies than on the store-bought poppers and sliders. So what was the point? I went back to buying poppers, and last year I "retired" a battered, black Bass Duster, which in two days had taken ten consecutive smallmouth bass—all over fifteen inches—without a miss. The bass were rising to flying ants. A small black Bass Duster resembles an ant about as much as a frog resembles a mayfly, but the bass assaulted that popper. They chewed off the legs and chipped most of the paint, and it was *still* catching fish. It was a champion, and afterward I enshrined that plucky little bug in its own plastic case, labeled and dated, something I have never done or felt like doing with any other popper or fly. The point was, I felt just as proud of that store-bought popper as of a fly I had tied myself. After all, do parents take less pride in their adopted children than in their biological offspring?

So, since I didn't care whose fly I caught fish on and did not take great pleasure in the act of tying, why did I continue to tie? To save money, I told myself, but that raised another question: how do you calculate the cost and value of homemade flies? For example, I bought a #2 Metz grizzly dry fly cape so many years ago I can't recall what I paid, but I'm sure it is fully depreciated, and it still contains more hackle than I will ever need. Likewise, how do you calculate the depreciation of fly tying tools? Or the $300 I recently spent on a custom-made tying table? Or the $50 for imported Jungle Cock? You need an actuarial table to figure all this out. And, trickiest of all, what about time? Is time a cost? You could cook the books and come up with any answer you wanted. Economics is simply not a satisfactory explanation for tying flies. There had to be other reasons.

Such as flexibility—flexibility astream and flexibility of pattern. I am convinced that there is only a single shade of orange suitable for a Gray Ghost, and that all streamers work better with marabou, and that Sparkle Hair has no place on a Black Ghost but, paradoxically, improves the Gray Ghost, and that peacock herl helps *all* flies. I have no scientific basis for saying this, but I am convinced that indulging my prejudices increases my confidence in the fly, which in turn improves my fishing.

Flexibility astream is easier: no matter how well you research a trip, eventually you will be caught by surprise. In 1982, on the West Fork of the Bitterroot River in Montana, big, ridiculous looking moths were dropping into the water, where sizeable, not ridiculous looking rainbows and cutthroats were slurping them up, to the exclusion of all else. I had nothing in my vest resembling those moths and the nearest fly shop was in Hamilton, and by the time I drove there and back, probably the frenzy would have ended. However, my fly tying kit was in the car, the vise fit the glove compartment door, and in a matter of minutes I was back, armed and dangerous. My crude Brown Wulffs were devastating, and they saved the day. I could cite several other examples in Idaho, Belize and even Maine.

But sometimes flexibility backfires, blows up in your face or simply leads to unanticipated consequences, and you have to rethink the whole question of motivation for tying flies all over again. And maybe the question is never settled. Perhaps motivation for tying flies continues to evolve, just as we do, over the course of our fishing lives.

One spring in the late 1980s three of us—Dan, Paul and I—were staying at Grant's Camps, fishing the Kennebago River for landlocked salmon. I'd known Dan for nearly twenty years and worked in the same office with Paul, a retired surgeon, for about five. Dan and Paul were former colleagues. In the office where Paul and I now worked, we got along, but there was an edgy competitiveness to our friendship. Also he and I had never fished together, though separately we had fished many of the same waters and both loved the Rangeley area.

The first morning the fishing was slow, but Dan had caught a couple, and over lunch he confided that the fish were holding deep, and that the best fly was a weighted Mickey Finn. Unfortunately, he had only one left, and Paul and I had none. However, I had brought my fly tying kit; I would be the hero. By the time we returned to the river for the evening's fishing, I had finished a dozen weighted Mickey Finns, an easy fly to tie.

Unfortunately, I had made a slight miscalculation and used heavy lead wire instead of fine, and I had used far too much of it. My Mickey Finns were very difficult to cast, and they were dangerous. If you ever managed to get one airborne, the back of your head, your shoulders and ear lobes were in serious jeopardy. These weren't flies; they were feathered bullets. They hurt! And they weren't barbless either. Yes, Paul was a surgeon, but this was not the time or place for him to demonstrate his skills. So I hurried along the river to warn him and Dan that, due to a slight manufacturing defect, the entire lot of Mickey Finns was being recalled. "Too much lead," I said.

"So I noticed," Paul said, nodding to the fly imbedded in the back of his vest.

I yanked it out with forceps. "Sorry about that," I said.

"Better a brooch than an earring."

"That's very generous of you."

"It was generous of you to give me the flies."

He was sincere. I could tell that the gift of the flies, however defective, registered with him.

Paul had a generous spirit, and at six foot, five inches he was the proverbial gentle giant. In his youth he had been "almost" an Olympian in the javelin. We never knew quite how close he actually came to qualifying for the games. The story changed slightly over the years. It "evolved." The older he got and the more he told it, the closer he came to qualifying. If only he had lived a few years longer…

Like many fishermen, Paul had a slight tendency to exaggerate his fishing exploits and it may have spilled over into other aspects of his life, which in his case was totally unnecessary. His real accomplishments were quite sufficient: skilled fly fisherman, competent watercolorist, Civil War historian, high school hoop legend (the "Giant of Franklin County"), teacher, community servant and "beloved physician," the exact phrase used by the local papers in the front-page article announcing his death earlier this year, more than a decade after our ill-fated trip to the Kennebago.

Poor vision had ended his surgical practice long ago and brought him to the office where he and I both worked. Even after he couldn't see to perform surgery, he continued to fish and tie flies, and every spring after our Kennebago debacle, he would give me a sample of flies he had tied over the winter. Devil Bugs were his specialty. Paul loved fishing brook trout ponds, where Devil Bugs were especially effective. He also gave me the combination to the lock on the canoe that he kept stashed on his favorite trout pond, a considerable gift. And last fall, just months before he died, he gave me a print of a watercolor he had done of a fly fisherman surveying a pond, in which one could see the ring of a rising fish. He said that the fisherman was me. He might have said the same to others; it didn't matter. A few months later, in the winter of '02, Paul died. His health had been shaky for a while. He smoked heavily and had survived a dozen recent operations, but his death was still such a surprise that at first some of us thought it might have been another fish story.

It wasn't; he's gone, but his watercolor still adorns the wall of my office, and I still have a few of his flies. I wish I'd kept more, but they were made to be fished. They were functional flies. Paul was a very good fly tier, not "collectible" good, but more than competent. He had his own unique tying

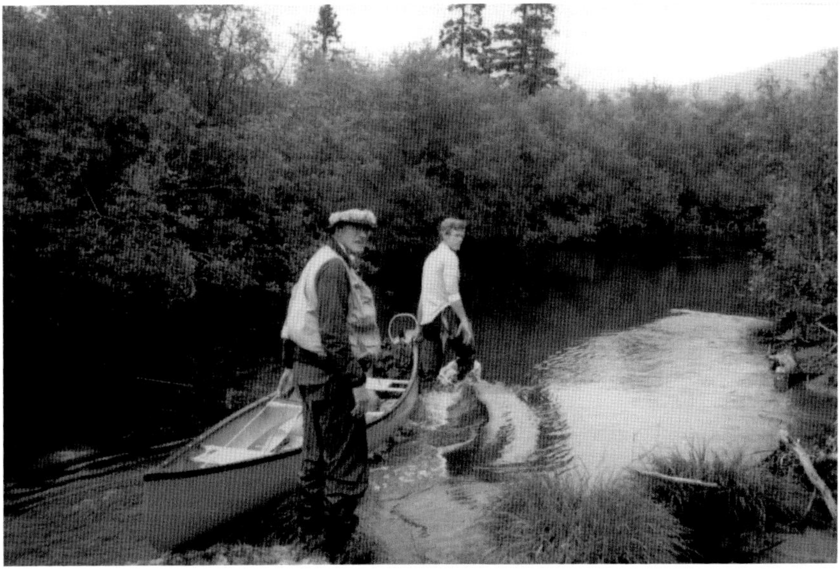

The late Paul Brinkman and Dan Onion on the upper reaches of the Kennebago River.

style, as do we all. His tying style, like his lifestyle, was one of "abundance," of "busyness." He was not a minimalist. His flies were neither underdressed nor overdressed. I would say they were amply dressed.

His death sadly but naturally made me reassess not just the value of his flies, but also the value of the defective ones I had given him years earlier. And it caused me to rethink my cocktail conversation with that lady years before that. Maybe the lady was more right than I realized; maybe it is about the fly and the fisherman, though not in the sense of the fly as an example of our cleverness.

No offense to the fish, but maybe sometimes our fishing is not always or only about the fish. Maybe later in our fishing lives the most important function of the fish is to bring fishermen together. And perhaps the homemade fly acts as the charged particle that, when transferred from fisherman to fisherman, creates a bond.

Or maybe not, but seeing it that way makes me feel better about spending $50 on Jungle Cock, or $300 on a table. Not to put too noble a spin on it, but in a way I'm doing it for my family and my extended family of fly-fishing friends, because I'm not just tying flies any more. I'm creating heirlooms.

Fishing Partners

Selecting a fishing partner is tricky business. Ultimately, as with many relationships, it comes down to luck and timing. Before Dan Onion was available to fish as frequently as I thought he should, I went through a series of interim partners, with varying results.

My first was Mahlon, a wiry native Mainer, a hunter and woodsman. He also owned a fly rod and fished a little. But once, on Spencer Stream in the middle of a caddis hatch, he found a logging chain. He became so excited by his discovery that he quit fishing and began lugging the chain back to the truck. The chain was enormous, each link about the size of a man's fish, but far heavier. He had trouble dragging the chain and his fly rod simultaneously and wondered, would I be kind enough to carry his fly rod for him? No, as a matter of fact, I wouldn't. "I came to fish," I said, "not to collect junk."

"But, Jim, a chain like this…"

"In case you haven't noticed, caddis flies are hatching. Trout are rising."

Another time on Parker Pond, he jumped ship to investigate a loon's nest. Normally, I'm tolerant of that sort of thing. I realize that fish do not exist in a vacuum, but in a great natural arena of birds, flowers, deer and so forth, and that when the fishing is slow we admire these lovely creations and remind ourselves, "It's just nice to be outside on a day like this." But that day the fishing was not slow; it was excellent, and one does not neglect good fishing for loons.

Later the same day, I moved to the stern of the canoe so that Mahlon could fish—fair is fair—and I would paddle. Mahlon would cast his little fly rod popper and gaze off at—I don't know what he was gazing at, because I was watching his popper; somebody had to. After he'd missed his third consecutive strike, I said, "Will you please pay attention!"

He turned and smiled. "Don't get so excited. It don't make that much difference to me," he said.

"In that case you sit back here."

Fine with him; we paddled ashore, switched positions and he never sat in the bow again, or even wanted to. In fact, we rarely fished together after that, even though we remained good friends until he moved to Eustis Ridge, because the town of Mt. Vernon, population of maybe one thousand, was just getting too crowded.

Mike was the husband of my then-wife's friend, a tenuous connection. I took Mike as a favor. He was a chef, a large man with mutton chops and a paunch. When he sat in the bow of my canoe, we bulldozed through the water like a barge. A bait fisherman, he was happy to try fly-fishing; so I took him for smallmouth on Torsey Pond, a place I fished often and felt protective about. Usually I wouldn't keep a fish unless it was injured, but—and here is where I went wrong—I hadn't told Mike that.

Often these initial outings aren't successful, but this one was, and by casting Sneaky Petes to the rocky shore, Mike soon hooked a nice two-pound smallmouth, which ran and jumped and did all the things smallmouth do, but was soon brought to hand. Mike wanted to keep it; so I strung it up—legal then, but not now. It was a good fish, his first on a fly rod, and he was rightfully proud, and I was a little proud myself that I could put a fly rod in his hand, show him fish and have him catch one. I did not like being too rigid about catch-and-release, particularly with a benchmark fish like his. After all, they're just fish, and human relationships come first. Up to a point.

Soon Mike caught another fish and kept that too. Fine, that pond could handle the occasional loss of two fish. Mike was excited; I was pleased. I took him home and, holding the two fish on the stringer, he ran into the house. A few moments later he ran back out, still carrying the fish. "I just wanted to show them to her," he said. "I kept them for you."

"Oh." I could see that he meant well; the fish were a gift to thank me for taking him, and I guess I should have said "you're welcome," but I couldn't. "I wish you'd told me you didn't want the fish," I said, eyeing the carcasses, no longer so beautiful now that they'd dried and faded.

"I wanted them for you."

"Next time just let me know, okay?"

But of course, there wasn't going to be any next time. Something always seemed to come up that interfered, and then he and his wife moved away and that was that.

Next came Phil, who did not kill fish—too messy to clean—but he loved to go and we caught many fish together, bass and landlocked salmon. The next year he bought an Orvis rod, and I thought, "Well now, this is getting serious." Then I found out that he had four deer rifles, but had never killed a deer; a Troy-bilt tiller for a tiny garden; and three bicycles—he liked collecting things—but only a single car for him and his wife. Soon transportation became a problem; he needed rides to and from his house, a distance of nearly twenty miles. And he began having trouble deciding how best to spend his time, riding his bike, planting flowers or fishing, as if the three activities were of equal importance to him. A dilettante, he wasn't serious. The second year we fished only a few times together and the third year only once, but that was enough to justify the rod, new canoe and outboard motor. Last I heard, he was pricing waders.

Cherie, a tall, pretty, blue-eyed blonde, was the least likely prospect for a fishing partner. Gender wasn't the issue. One of my favorite fishing companions is my sister Ida, who at the age of fourteen was independent on the water, and now fishes the Chesapeake commercially.

The issue was Cherie's age and inexperience. At the age of thirty she had never fished. Her husband didn't fish, her father didn't fish; he sailed. Her brother sailed; she sails; my brother sails, and as a rule, sailors are very different from fishermen. They are not better or worse; just different. Sailing is generally a clean, blood-free sport, and no matter how hard we try to keep our fly-fishing blood free, we fail. Fish die. So that winter evening when Cherie asked me when I was going to take her fly-fishing, I said, "Preferably after the snow melts." If she was still interested then, we'd see.

By spring she had read two fly-fishing books, bought hip boots, had practiced casting with a borrowed rod and had even taught herself to tie a few knots. She was raring to go. We started with smallmouth bass. If they didn't excite her, I wanted to know and know soon.

Our first trip was a week too early on a cold, windy day, and the one fish I caught was as lethargic as an ice cube, and died before I could release him. Cherie caught nothing but did not complain about the cold or the poor fishing. "It was still fun," she said, as she helped lug the canoe back to the truck. The lady was a trouper.

Finally real spring arrived, in Maine a thin sliver of time between mud season and summer. One warm, calm evening we fished the rocky islands

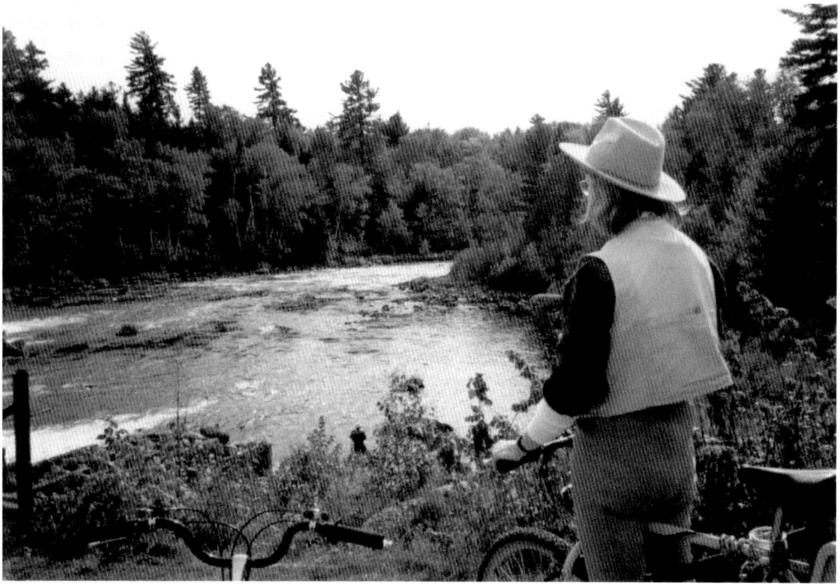

After a long bike ride in, Cherie Wenzel checks out the Rapid River.

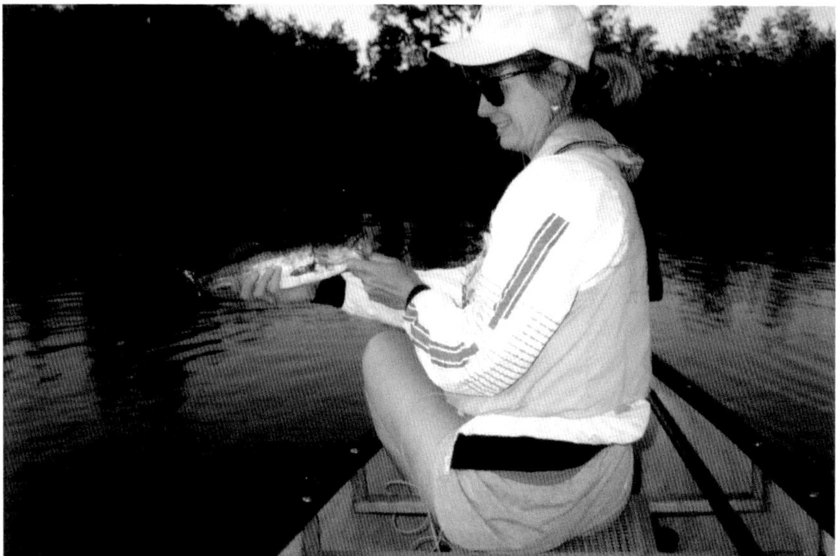

Cherie with a Morse Pond largemouth bass.

of Parker Pond. In the sunlight, there's a Caribbean clarity to Parker; the mossy submerged boulders resemble emerald-colored coral heads. Tall pines usually hold osprey, and on one island there's an eagle's nest. And the shoreline always holds fish. We caught plenty, but the last came after dark, illuminated by a full moon. The fish jumped, shook and sent a spray like a shower of diamonds.

Then it was summer and time for Morse Pond, a quiet carry-in pond with no boat launch and not a single camp along its wooded shoreline. The pond is L-shaped, fertile, weedy, with a wealth of insects and largemouth bass. Cherie loved the fishing, the solitude, the silence and the wildlife—the loons; the turtles arranged according to size on a fallen log like a toy store display; and the startled black ducks leaping loudly up from the cattails, none of which she let distract her from her fishing. Because Morse is but fifteen minutes away, we fished it frequently, and it never let us down.

Soon, too soon, it was fall, and time to move upcountry to the Kennebago River for landlocked salmon. It was a ninety-minute drive, then a two-mile bike ride and then a hike over the semblance of a trail littered with fallen timber, dry-kill, that forces detours through dense thickets of small spruce and fir. The footing is unreliable, and the fishing is hit or miss. Our first trip was on a bright, sunny day, lovely foliage, but the worst possible conditions for salmon. Cherie never complained about the weather, the walking, the fishing or even her companion, who was a veritable Job. "Why couldn't we get just a little cloud cover? Is that too much to ask?" Evidently it was.

And then, near midday, at a shallow, rather unspectacular, pool, a nice salmon materialized out of ledge and shadow, took my fly and streaked toward the tail of the pool. If he'd continued to the heavy water, he would've broken off at once, but it goes against a salmon's instincts to swim downstream in fall. So he turned and raced back to the head of the pool and leaped high into the air, right in front of our eyes. "He's beautiful!" Cherie yelled, as excitedly as if the fish had been on her line instead of mine.

He jumped so often that he wore himself out, and I soon slid him into the shallows and netted him. He measured eighteen inches. "Do you want to keep him?" I asked. Then you could legally keep one fish.

"Not if it's a female," she said.

"It's a male." I knew she wanted to take a fish back to her husband. Who wouldn't? It's how we sometimes justify our time away from home.

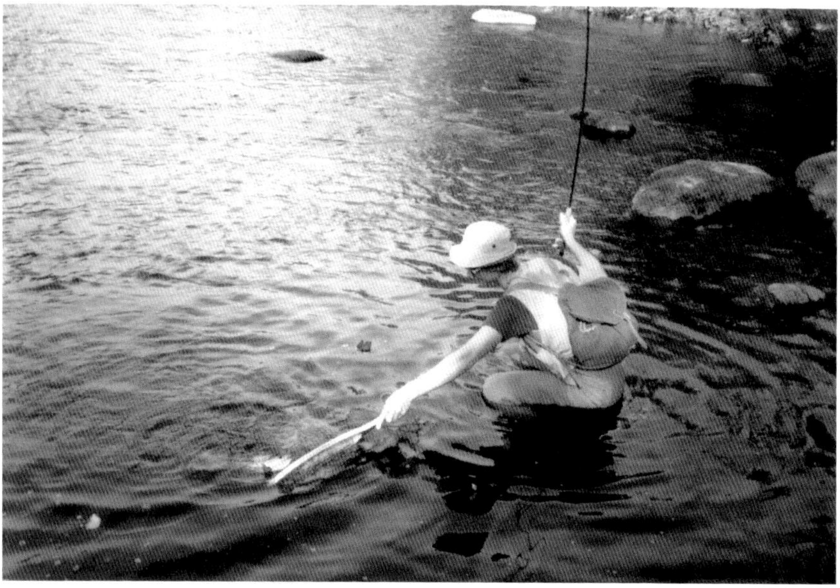

Cherie netting a landlocked salmon on the Kennebago River.

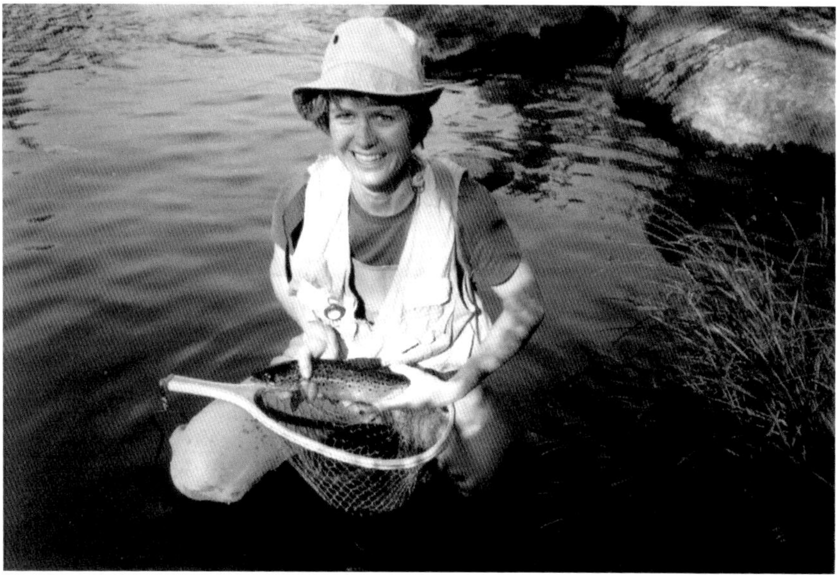

Cherie about to release the same fish.

She was quiet for a moment. "Oh, let him go," she said. "He's too pretty to kill."

I revived and released the fish, and he shot away and disappeared in water so shallow it hardly seemed adequate to conceal such a bright, shining fish, but such are the mysteries of fish and rivers.

Cherie and I sat in the now-warm sun and felt pleased. A single fish can change a day from miserable to memorable. A relationship can be transformed from casual friendship to something like a partnership based on shared values—she spared the fish. It was not a test, but it was, I believed, a pivotal moment. I thought perhaps that I had found an enduring fishing partner, but I was wrong.

We fished together a few more years, but then Cherie had a son, Luke, and understandably her priorities changed. Three years later I had the privilege of taking Luke, elfin and adorable, on his first fishing trip on Morse Pond, along with his mother, of course. We even caught a fish; but for me it was a bittersweet experience—my first fishing trip with Luke, but one of my last with Cherie, and I knew it. Luke is fifteen now, a teenager! He plays soccer and guitar; he snowboards, lifts weights and "occasionally," according to his mother, looks at girls, but he does not fish and, sadly, neither does his mother.

And so it goes. People come to fishing for many reasons; some drift away, but those who stay do so for a single reason: the fish. It's as simple and as complicated as that.

Guiding the Guide

To have a registered Maine guide as a friend is an honor, and to have a master guide, such as my friend Stuart, is an even higher honor and a privilege. The friendship comes with perks: a free drift-boat trip down the East Outlet of the Kennebec, wade-fishing Stuart's favorite pool on the Roach River, free use of his Atlantic salmon flies and even homemade hard cider from apples picked from the guide's own orchard, pressed by the guide's own hands—a high honor indeed. The trouble came when I tried to reciprocate.

One spring day I suggested that Stuart come with me to Torsey Pond for smallmouth bass. Stuart, of course, did not fish for bass. "None of your friends have to know," I said. "Besides, what else are you doing for the next few hours?"

He had no answer. We were sitting in my living room discussing fish, which was a great wintertime activity, but winter was over. We loaded my canoe and thirty minutes later we were cruising the rocky shoreline of Torsey Pond. I paddled from the stern; Stuart sat up front casting Sneaky Petes to the shallows. Soon he hooked a nice smallmouth, about fifteen inches, and in the clear water the coppery fish shone yellow, green, then golden brown. Stuart lipped the fish, turned and smiled and I took his picture. I'm glad I caught that ephemeral moment on film—a happy Stuart—because the minute I resumed paddling, Stuart started complaining.

"Where're we going? Why are we leaving this spot? I like this spot."

"This time of year," I patiently explained, "the fish are not schooled up. They're scattered along the shoreline."

"We just found fish and you're leaving them?"

"This whole shoreline is so productive that I call it the 'Gold Coast.'" I had fished Torsey Pond for twenty years. Stuart had never fished that

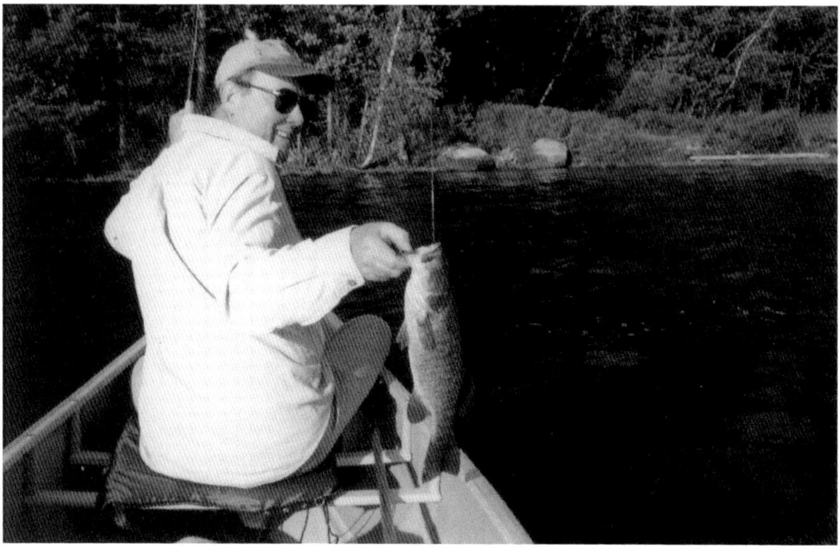

Master Guide Stuart Smith and a happy moment on Torsey Pond.

pond before, but he knew where he wanted to fish: right where he caught that first one.

Finally I asked, "How do you like it when your sports tell you where to fish?"

That silenced him temporarily. We continued along the shoreline, but he caught nothing. I thought he did it just to spite me. "Put your popper right against the rocks," I said. "Don't be afraid to get it too shallow."

He shifted in his seat and tried to stretch his legs. He's a tall man, and my new lightweight canoe has low seats for stability.

"I hate canoes," he said.

"How can anyone 'hate' a canoe?" My Lincoln Sunrise was my pride and joy: fifteen and a half feet and only forty-eight pounds; Kevlar with a beautiful hardwood trim and cane seats, low cane seats.

"Canoes are uncomfortable," he said. His knees were up near his chest; to prove his point he touched them with his chin.

"Okay, we'll go ashore."

I pulled into a gravel beach where Stuart could stretch his legs and complain in comfort. Then we headed back along the same shoreline, and soon we were back where we had started, at which point Stuart promptly caught another fish. Then another. "I told you so," he said, laughing, as the fish jumped. I was so happy to see him catch fish that I ignored the insult. This time we didn't move far from that area, and in a couple of hours he caught seven legal smallmouths to sixteen inches, an honest two pounds (a "conversational" three), all on the indomitable Sneaky Pete. Then it was time to go.

Paddling in, Stuart turned to me and said, "I don't know what you're used to, but most of my clients would be happy with this fishing."

I could hardly believe my ears: praise from the master guide. "I hope mine would be too," I said.

I didn't see Stuart again until the middle of July. He had been upcountry fishing and guiding. Now it was hot, the hatches were over, the waters were low and the trout and salmon had retreated to the spring holes. Stuart came by to commiserate.

"That's what I hate about Maine," he said. "You get a few weeks in the spring, and then nothing until September." He laughed his joyless laugh that translated roughly into, "No matter what you do, you are screwed."

"Speak for yourself," I said. "I've been having a heck of a time. Any night I want, several nice fish, top-water, ten minutes from home."

"Bass?" He looked at me over his glasses.

"Yes, bass. You have a problem with that?"

"I thought you told me the bass went deep, that you couldn't catch them this time of year."

"Smallmouth, yes, they're tough now. Largemouth on the other hand…but I realize that sort of fishing is beneath you. And I respect that. We all have our standards."

"You're catching largemouth now?"

I nodded. "It's not fast fishing. I've had better years, but I get a couple or three good ones each time I go."

"What's a 'good' one?"

"Sixteen to seventeen inches. Two and a half to three pounds." Stuart knew that I actually weighed and measured my fish.

"That's not bad."

"Well, on surface poppers I find it rather enjoyable."

"Well, what the hell, let's go some time," he blurted out in a burst of bonhomie.

"You gonna behave?" He pretended not to know what I was talking about.

I love Morse Pond. It is nearby, predictable and it is private—no houses, no motorboats. Most importantly, it is a bass factory, a rich biological stew of aquatic vegetation, insects and fish. I have the use of a canoe on Morse. It's not as light as my canoe, which means the seats are higher, and Stuart was not quite so folded and cramped.

We went on July 19, 2001, and as predicted, in about two hours, we took three sixteen-inch largemouth bass. There were explosive takes, strong fights, somersaulting leaps and mad dives into weeds. Unfortunately, even though I sat in the stern and cast only occasionally, I caught all three fish. Stuart caught a couple of small ones, but lost the only good fish he hooked. It is hard to explain how this happens. Well, it is hard for me to explain; it was easy for Stuart: life sucked, bass fishing sucked, Morse Pond sucked. "That was almost as much fun as mowing the lawn," he said. The line was stolen from a local outdoor writer, but Stuart said it like he meant it.

I didn't see Stuart again until the fall; it was probably just as well. Insult Morse Pond, and you insult me.

In September, Stuart fishes the Moosehead area; I fish Rangeley. In late October, he showed up again and once again to commiserate: low water, lousy fishing, global warming, crowded rivers, 9/11. The world was going to hell, just like he had always suspected.

This time I had to agree. "It probably is going to hell," I said, "but I'm not going with it. I'm going fishing."

He looked puzzled. "What's open now? Shawmut? That place reeks."

I shook my head. "Not Shawmut. I have a new river: the Androscoggin."

He laughed. Historically, the Androscoggin was one of the most polluted rivers in America.

"Laugh if you want to, but I've seen some mighty nice rainbows and browns come out of there this fall."

I showed him a newspaper article and told him my own experiences. "It's open through November," I said.

The warm fall, the curse of our September, was a blessing in November, and it was a very mild November morning when Stuart and I drifted the Androscoggin. It was seven miles of deep runs, pools and riffles and braided currents and chutes, against a background of pine, softwood and in places sheer granite cliffs. The only leaves that hadn't fallen were the tan ones of ash and poplar and the darker brown of red oak. Except for a pair of kayakers, we had the river to ourselves.

Stuart was not enthralled. "What's the water temperature?"

I made a quick check. "Forty-two degrees." I should have lied.

"I can't believe I am fly-fishing in forty-two-degree water," he said. "The fish are dormant!"

"Don't give up too soon," I said. We'd barely gotten started. "The day is young."

"That's what bothers me. Do we really have to go the whole seven miles?"

"You don't have to, but I am."

He was sullen.

We beached the canoe and wade fished a large pool in the main current. I caught a diminutive rainbow, maybe six inches long. I held it up for Stuart to see. “That one wasn’t dormant.”

“A dink.”

“True, but it is a very important dink, because nobody is stocking fish this size. Do you know what that means? This may be a wild fish!”

“Whoopee.”

We fished through the middle of the day, lunching on a sunny island beside a gorgeous pool, where unfortunately we caught nothing. Stuart was inconsolable. He stood, stretched and looked around, and sounding like Chief Joseph laying down his arms forever, announced, “I will never fish this river again.” Mercifully, November days in Maine are short. Sunset about 4:30, dark before 5:00.

In the early afternoon, blue-winged olives hatched, and in a long, straight glide trout began to rise. They should have saved the day, but instead only served to make things worse. Stuart was in the bow; I positioned the canoe above the fish so that he could cast down to them, but either the canoe or his casts spooked every fish. We had not a single take. “I hate this type of fishing,” he said. “Frigging finicky trout.”

“You need to be more careful with your casts,” I said. “These aren’t brookies.” The wrong thing to say to a master guide, but it had been a long day.

Then in the same stretch we located fish rising closer to shore. “We can wade to those,” I said.

We came ashore below the rising fish and waded until we both had fish above us and to our right. Not a bad setup if you had the right fly, a size #18 or #20 blue-winged olive, which I did. Soon I took a ten-inch rainbow, a shiny, silver, chunky fish that jumped in the sinking sunlight.

“Another dink?” Stuart asked.

“I wouldn’t call it that,” I said, admiring and then releasing the beautiful little trout. “I’d call it a nice chunky rainbow.”

Another fish was rising just above where I took the first, and soon I hooked him too, an eleven-inch brown, beautifully marked, buttery and polka-dotted.

“Dink city, huh?” Stuart said.

“Call it what you want,” I said. “All I know is, I am catching rising fish on dry flies in November in Maine! And I am having fun.”

“I hate this type of fishing,” Stuart said.

“You might enjoy it more if you caught something. You want to borrow a blue-winged olive?”

"Nah, I'm ready to go."

"Come on, I'll bring one down to you."

He reeled in; he'd had enough. We called it a day and paddled in the fading light to the take out.

The kayakers, a guide from L.L. Bean and his out-of-state sport, arrived at the takeout just before we did and were loading up. Years ago Stuart had worked at Bean's. He and the guide, Van, compared notes, talked shop and then discussed this river and their day of fishing. Van and his sport hadn't done much either, but Van fished that river regularly, and in his understated way allowed as how there were some good fish in that river. Rainbows and browns measured in pounds, not inches. Slowly, during the course of the conversation, Stuart's expression changed. He listened with interest. He and Van reminded me of a couple of physicians conferring over a difficult clinical problem, not which medicines to use, but which flies and what time of year? A lot of information was exchanged in clipped jargon, guide talk.

Eavesdropping on that conversation, I came to realize that Stuart's problem was not really with the river or the fishing. His problem was with me. My taking him fishing, instead of the other way around, disrupted the natural order of things. He sensed it, even if he couldn't or didn't put it into words. I was practicing without a license. I was a quack. As a matter of pride and principle, Stuart was not going to be cured by a quack, a charlatan. He'd rather stay sick, or in this case, unhappy. However, if another guide endorsed the river, that was different. Van said that this river fished better in late September and October, or even in the spring, when there were some heavy mayfly hatches, along with caddis and stonefly. That provided Stuart with a diagnosis: the "wrong time." I, the quack, the quasi guide, the poseur, had brought him fishing at the wrong time of the year. Any knowledgeable person would've known you weren't going to catch decent fish in forty-two-degree water.

"How come Van didn't know?" I asked later.

"Van was *paid*!" he said.

That explained it. If you were a pro, a guide, and it was your job, and if some flatlander was foolish enough to pay you to take them, you did it. Same as building contractors and carpenters worked in the cold, or a doctor went out in the middle of the night. It was your job and you did it. But what you *didn't* do, Stuart implied but was kind enough not to say, was let some rank amateur drag you down a frigid river for a couple of dinks and then try and tell you it was *fun*. Neither of us would let *that* happen again.

Further Scenes with the Master Guide

One snowy Sunday afternoon, Stuart Smith stormed into my living room, garrulous and excited. He had just finished Thomas McGuane's *The Longest Silence* and wanted to share his enthusiasm.

"The guy is *so* good," he said, as he draped his large frame over the love seat across from me.

"Yes, he is very good," I said. We both liked McGuane. Everybody likes McGuane.

"When you read his stuff, doesn't it make you just want to shoot yourself?"

I said, "No. It makes me want to shoot you for coming into *my* house raving about another writer."

He cackled. "You know I like your stuff, Jim. It's just that McGuane, he takes it to a whole other level."

"You're just making it worse, Stuart."

He laughed and sputtered even harder. He thought I was joking. His thinning hair was mussed; he wore faded jeans and ancient Bean boots. He used the untucked tail of his green flannel shirt to clean his wire-rimmed glasses. In his little green cap, he reminds me of Fidel Castro, but without it he looks like a college professor. In fact, he was an English major, and he remains a voracious reader and a fierce social and literary critic.

I asked, "How would you like it if I came over to your house and started raving about what a great guide Mark Evans was?"

Stuart winced; I'd hurt him, and I meant to. "Yeah, Dan and I had quite a day with him up on the East Outlet. Caught some really nice salmon. A lot more than I caught with you. Though I certainly appreciate you taking me. Don't think I don't."

He wasn't cackling any more. "Mark Evans is just the type of guide I don't like."

"Why? Because he catches fish?"

"Naw, he's so aggressive. It's go, go, go all the time."

"I like aggressive guides. They get results. All John and I got with you were dinks. You said that water was 'pooched out.' Well, lemme tell you, either that river has made a miraculous comeback or Mark Evans is one amazing guide."

"Yeah, I remember that day," Stuart said, recalling our trip down the East Outlet. "You and big John were fishing streamers in the middle of a caddis hatch! I had to *tell* you change flies." He thought that was pretty funny, his dumb sports not even noticing the hatch.

"Yeah, well maybe we should've ignored your advice and kept fishing streamers. We might have caught something. With Mark we didn't worry about a hatch. We went down and dirty. It worked too."

Stuart paused for a minute. "Did you know that Mark once wanted me to work out of their shop?"

"No, as a matter of fact, I didn't know that."

"He wanted me to do the whole river, but I could never work for him."

Stuart was very particular about whom he worked for, and where he worked and when. I had gotten even, and I had gotten him off the subject of Thomas McGuane. Now it was time to make up. "Come downstairs," I said. "I want to show you something."

He unfolded himself from the sofa and followed me into the basement, where I showed him my new fly tying table. I had designed it myself and had it built partly in response to a comment Stuart had made about my previous setup, which consisted of two TV tables pushed together and covered with plastic. "No wonder you don't like to tie flies," he'd said, and I realized that he had a point. So when my boys went off to college and I had more room, I got a table built, with which I was rather pleased. Stuart, however, was less impressed. "How much did it cost?" he asked, after he had given it a critical once-over.

"$300."

"$300! Jeesum!!"

"What'd you think it would cost?"

He rubbed his chin. "I don't know, maybe $100."

I laughed. Stuart was a little out of touch with economic realities. "Get real," I said. "It's custom made."

"It's plywood!"

"Just the cubby, and that can be removed, or painted." That *was* a mistake, and hadn't been my idea. It was the builder's idea to make the cubbies larger.

He still wasn't convinced. "I don't know, Jim. $300..." $300 seemed like a lot to Stuart because he wasn't working at the moment.

"Yeah, but you've got to figure those $300 are amortized over my lifetime, factoring in the increased productivity due to better working conditions—hell, it'll pay for itself in a couple of years."

"If you say so, Jim."

We went back upstairs. I made coffee and we resumed our conversation about fishing and writing about fishing. It's an important subject to us: Stuart and I met because of a story that I had written about a maniacal Maine fly fisherman who became so obsessed with building an indoor river that it cost him his marriage and more. The story somehow spoke to Stuart, told him that I understood the powerful, sometimes self-destructive forces that drove one to a life of fishing. If I couldn't actually live that life myself, I could at least imagine it and see it as a good thing, and that meant something to Stuart. And, of course, that he was moved by something that I wrote meant a lot to me. It was the basis of our friendship, an abrasive, argumentative friendship, to be sure, but also surprisingly resilient.

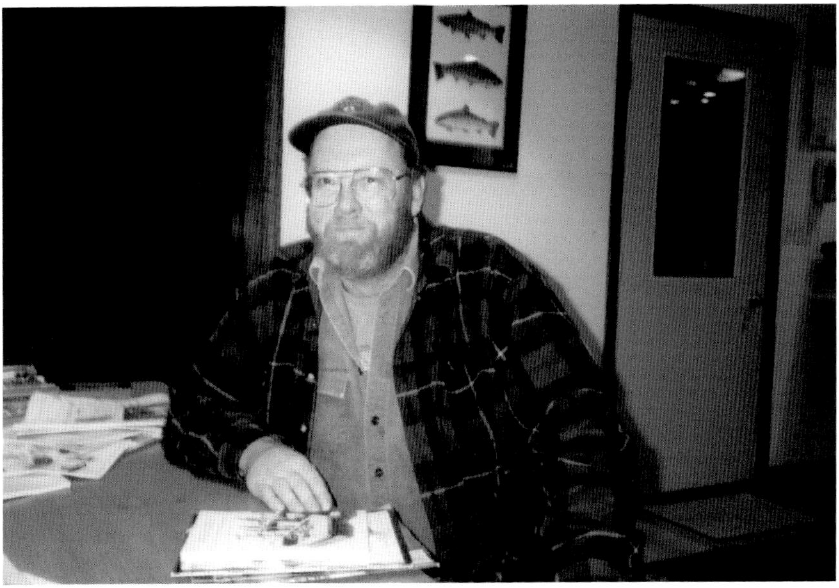

The master guide in the author's dining room, discussing life, literature and fishing.

Outside my living room window the snow piled up. Lovejoy Pond was a white palimpsest of footprints, animal tracks and snowmobile and ski trails. Stuart and I wistfully looked forward to ice out, and the *Kennebec Journal*'s annual red quill article, a true harbinger of spring. We chatted about new books on Carrie Stevens and Flyrod Crosby, two Maine icons, and old ones by another well-known writer whom Stuart found "redundant."

To which I said, "As much as he writes he *has* to be redundant. Better to repeat yourself once in a while than waste good material."

"Spoken like a true writer," Stuart said.

"That's the nicest thing you've said all day. Guess you were overdue."

For that I refilled his coffee, and we compared notes on a rerelease by Gifford Pinchot and new books by Scott Sadil, David Detweiler and Jack Hemingway. We argued and we laughed, but all within the context of a shared faith—fly-fishing and its amazing ability to move so many people to so many words, none of which completely conveys what it is we want to hear or say. So the work goes on.

The Master Guide Takes Early Retirement

Ordinary work does not come naturally to master guides. Nor should it. Guiding is a vocation, a calling. Some men, such as Stuart Smith, are born to fish and to lead other men to fish.

Stuart's work history is what some might call "checkered," but to a fisherman it is exemplary. His steadiest work was a sixteen-year stint guiding at the Megantic Club on the headwaters of the Kennebago River in western Maine. This involved rowing elderly, wealthy folk around Big Island Pond for native brookies, but also required hiking to more remote ponds where the club kept boats. Then more rowing and paddling. Naturally over the course of sixteen years, all this hiking and rowing and paddling of old people took a toll on Stuart's health, his feet in particular. He suffered from pes planus, a painful condition that, in fact, disqualified him from military service—4-F. Eventually the same condition caught up with him at the Megantic Club and led to his retirement, but mercifully did not prevent him from fishing altogether.

Periodically Stuart would bravely attempt to rejoin the workforce, usually with unhappy results. An array of natural, political and medical forces conspired against him. For example, his career in the fishing department of a famous Maine sporting goods company was thwarted by his "brutal supervisor," a total "jerk." Stuart, a man of principle, would not work for jerks.

One summer Stuart operated the sightseeing launch that ran between the mainland and Mount Kineo on Moosehead Lake. This meant long hours on his surgically repaired feet, pitching and yawing on seas that were often as rough as ocean waters. Soon his feet began to ache; then a knee failed. Just how many body parts was he supposed to sacrifice for summer people?

In the year 2000 he had his heart set on a census-taker job, only to be rendered ineligible by an ancient, trivial and "totally unfounded," but sadly unresolved, legal issue.

"Couldn't you get that cleared up?" I asked.

"Not without going all the way to Washington, D.C.," he said. "And it's already too late for the census job."

"Yeah, but for the future."

He shrugged as if to say, "In such an unjust system, in such an unfair world, why bother?"

At that time Stuart lived in a duplex less than a mile from me in Wayne, Maine. One summer morning as I drove past Stuart's place, I saw six unmarked black vehicles parked out front and eight serious looking men in flak jackets milling around in the street. Some of the jackets bore large yellow letters, "ATF" or "DEA." One man wearing rubber gloves was jimmying a window.

I slid to a halt, and thought, "Maybe there's more to this 'unresolved legal issue' than I realized." I exited my car, and with both hands in plain sight, cautiously approached an armed man, who turned to me and glared. I showed him my empty hands and asked, "Is Stuart okay?"

"Is he the big guy?"

"Yes."

"Yeah, he's fine. This has nothing to do with him."

"Can I speak to him?" I asked.

The officer hesitated, clearly unaccustomed to being interrupted in the middle of a big operation. "Yeah, I guess," he finally said.

One officer was crawling through the jimmied window when I knocked on the front door and Stuart—or the ghost of Stuart—appeared, looking as pale and sickly as anyone I'd ever seen who wasn't hospitalized. "You all right?" I asked. "You look a little pale around the gills."

His dilated eyes darted suspiciously in all directions. "Well, it's not the best way to start the day," he said. "Guys in flak jackets banging on your back door."

"Yeah, but they're not after you. I already asked. It's the other guy."

"I know," he said, but he didn't sound convinced. Clearly this episode just confirmed his already bleak Kafka-esque worldview.

Later, when he'd recovered from the shock, but not from the absurdity, he elaborated. "Six cars, eight men, four hours! Do you how any idea how much that stupid operation cost the American taxpayers?"

"A lot?"

"I could live for six months on what the government wasted on that stupid drug bust. And what was it all for? A couple of ounces of pot! Well, aren't we all a lot safer now that that's off the street?" Then he emitted a long, nihilistic cackle, his signature laugh, as identifiable as a birdsong.

Then one day in the late winter of 2002 a happy, animated, upbeat Stuart—I barely recognized him—burst through the front door. A friend of his had just opened a fishing lodge on Bristol Bay in Alaska, and he wanted Stuart to guide for the lodge and wanted Stuart's girlfriend Marion to do the cooking. "Between the two of us, we can make enough money to get us through the winter, maybe longer." A winter without having to work was a sign of a successful summer and a point of pride.

"Hey, that's great," said I, happy to see him catch a break. He showed me the impressive brochures of vast expanses of wilderness and water. "I have a question, though. Have you ever even *been* to Alaska?" Naively, I had assumed that Alaskan guides spent years in the bush, learning the waters and honing their skills.

Stuart laughed, but it was a happy laugh. "No, I've never been, but you go a week early to learn the water, and the lodge-owner takes care of the guide's license. So it's all set."

"Fantastic!" In the decade or so that I had known Stuart, this was the most optimistic that I had ever seen him. In retrospect, I should have recognized it as a warning sign.

Shortly before he departed, Stuart stopped in to say goodbye and borrow a book. Then he was off. Five weeks later I received my book and a letter from Alaska. It said, in part, "I guess the lesson is, if something sounds too good to be true, it is."

Everything was awful: the camps were not even completed; he wasn't guiding; he was doing *carpentry* and *plumbing*, jacking up cabins and installing doors. The river was too high to fish, the mosquitoes were three times the size of Maine mosquitoes and the windows had no screens, until he put them in himself. It rained constantly, and when it wasn't raining the sun shone twenty-plus hours a day. Always a light sleeper, Stuart found that much sunshine "obnoxious." And so far there weren't any fishing clients.

I briefly considered writing him back and trying to bolster his spirits, but knew better. My pep talk would be added to his litany of complaints: not only were the mosquitoes huge, the river high and the housing awful, but his so-called friends fed him platitudes and homilies.

The next time I saw Stuart was September in the parking lot of the Fayette Country Store. "Hey, I didn't know you were back," I said.

"I've been back," he said. "We only stayed five weeks. We've been holed up at Moosehead."

"Oh. I got your letter, and I meant to write, but, well…"

"I wasn't expecting you to write. I just wanted to return the book."

It was a warm sunny day—a late summer dry spell—and we leaned against the bed of his truck, basking in the pleasant weather. "I guess the lodge wasn't quite all it was cracked up to be, hunh?"

He emitted a long, bitter laugh of dismay. "It wasn't just the lodge," he said, as if I'd grossly underestimated the degree of misery to which he'd been subjected. "I wasn't even guiding, but the worst thing was that frigging sun. There was just no getting away from it."

"You didn't sleep well?"

"Did you see that movie *Insomnia*?"

"Yes, as a matter of fact, I did." A detective played by Al Pacino travels to Alaska to solve a crime and is harassed by unremitting daylight, though he does manage to solve the crime.

"Remember Al Pacino putting blankets over all the windows? Well, that was me."

"I wouldn't like that either," I said. "So now what?"

"I don't know. There's no water in Maine."

"I know where there's water," I said. "The Androscoggin has water."

Stuart hated that water. "A friend of mine fished up there this spring. He didn't catch a single fish over twelve inches," he said, as if that settled that. If *his* friend couldn't catch a decent fish, why bother? His friends were pros.

I didn't argue. It was foolish to argue when Stuart was on the descending limb of his worldview. I'd catch him later, after the weather had cooled and he'd spent some quality time camped on the Roach River with his hard-core fishing buddies.

"You know, I just had a birthday," Stuart said.

"Hey, Happy Birthday! Let me buy you a beer."

"That's not what I'm getting at. The thing is, I just turned fifty," he said, making fifty sound extremely old. "My feet are starting to bother me again, my knee is killing me and now I need gallbladder surgery." He laughed a sad, somewhat philosophical laugh, resigned to his fate.

"Just one thing after another," I said, finally hitting the right note. I knew he didn't have health insurance. Even working guides couldn't afford health insurance.

"I think my body is trying to tell me something," Stuart said.

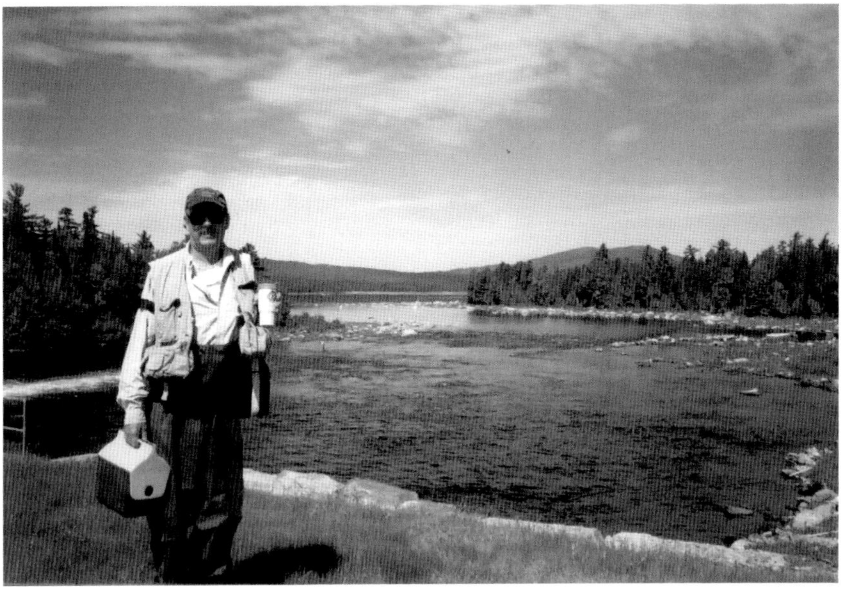

Master Guide Stuart Smith at Upper Dam, home water of the legendary Carrie Stevens.

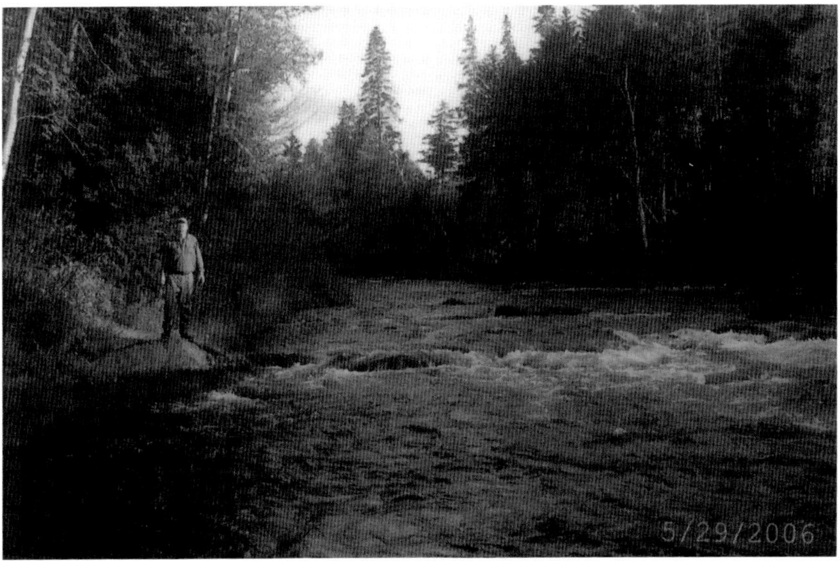

The master guide patrols his beloved Roach River.

"Yeah, maybe it is."

"Might be time to hang it up."

"Just might be."

We said our goodbyes and went our separate ways. Whatever he did next—retirement or one final stab at the workforce—I knew that he would continue fishing. Nothing was going to interfere with that. He could have both feet amputated and he would keep fishing. Because Stuart is a fly fisherman in its purest form. He is a true "fishing bum," which among fly fishermen is a huge compliment.

By comparison, my fishing life is a compromise. I'm an avid fisherman with a medical degree, a part-time job, two children and a writing habit. The world is full of avid, compromised fly fishermen, but honest-to-goodness, full-blooded fishing bums are few and far between. Even John Gierach, the writer with whom the term "fishing bum" is most famously connected, is not as pure as Stuart. Stuart has the education and verbal skills to write, but he has steadfastly resisted the pressure—including pressure from me—to transform his fishing experience into literature. He has kept it clean. He has successfully resisted *all* the pressure that society applies to anyone who dares to take his fishing seriously.

Stuart has the purity of vision of an artist. Not a painter or a writer, because Stuart's work leaves no permanent residue. Like dance or music, Stuart's fishing is performance art, as ephemeral and elegant as ballet. And just because there's not an audience doesn't mean it isn't art.

Bright Fish, Nice City

In the fall of 1986 our Trout Unlimited chapter set out to clean the west bank of the Kennebec River below the Edwards Dam in Augusta, Maine. Though few of us ever fished that section, our chapter bore the river's name, and therefore, we felt obligated to tidy up her much sullied shores.

The Kennebec has a long, storied and somewhat sordid history. Over the centuries it has served as a source of electricity and food, a transportation route, a conduit for logs, and also as a sewer and a dump. But in the last decade the log drives had ended, pollution had been reduced and the river was coming back to life. Amazingly, it still held fish.

It was a cloudy, cool, October day when we arrived. The river's bank was a slippery mix of ledge and mud, littered with tires, bottles, cans, grocery carts, assorted auto parts, coils of wire and other unidentifiable pieces of scrap metal—several truckloads of material. The tide was low, and even as we removed the most recent layer of debris, we could see intriguing wakes at the shallow outlet of Bond Brook. The river was known to have a small run of Atlantic salmon of controversial origin. Native fish? Penobscot strays? Escapees from a coastal aquaculture operation? People could not agree, but every fall a few dozen fish would stubbornly ascend the Kennebec until they hit the Augusta dam, at which point they would turn left into Bond Brook. A few people actually fished for them, but fishing in downtown Augusta had never appealed to me.

A decade earlier I had devoted a couple of seasons to the pursuit of Atlantic salmon in Downeast Maine. I never caught a single one. The closest I came was discovering a prehistoric fishing site on the banks of the Machias River. On the basis of a plummet and projectile points, the state archaeologist determined that the site was last occupied about three thousand years ago—an extreme example of "you should've been here yesterday." But that experience at least taught me what an Atlantic salmon river ought to look like, and it did not look like the Kennebec in downtown Augusta.

Also, I had once seen a slide show by a very famous fishing author on "His Majesty," *Salmo salar*, filmed in England: gorgeous shots of lush green countryside, meandering streams, gleaming salmon, nattily attired gillies; castles and aristocrats—in other words, nothing whatsoever like Augusta. A slide show of salmon fishing in Augusta would feature the underbellies of two rusty bridges, the abandoned Edwards Mill, the backside of downtown, parking lots, old buildings, an adult video store, a seedy bar, a soup kitchen and not a single aristocrat, just a few locals down on their luck. And to fully capture the flavor of the local fishing culture, there would have to be at least one unsavory character peering down from the Bond Brook bridge, an empty grocery cart in one hand, a length of rope in the other. (Though I've never seen the technique described in the fishing literature, as I understand it, the cart is lowered or dropped upside down onto spawning salmon.) The soundtrack of such a video would include not birdsongs, but traffic noises, sirens, horns and booming subwoofers.

On the other hand, according to the experts in our TU chapter, those really were Atlantic salmon bulldozing around practically at our ankles, and after all those miles I'd driven to the Denny's, the Machias and Penobscot without even *seeing* a fish, didn't I deserve to catch at least one salmon in my life, even under less than ideal circumstances? Wouldn't it be ironic, after all that effort, to find what I had so diligently sought right under my nose, within three minutes of where I worked?

So the very next day after work, rod in hand, I returned to the cleanup site, which, despite the truckloads of debris we had removed, still did not look particularly inviting. No matter. I donned waders and rigged my rod with the same degree of seriousness and respect I would have brought to Cascapedia, Restigouche or Test. Fly selection presented a problem. Unable to locate my old Sucrets box of Atlantic salmon flies, I settled on a Warden's Worry, a local bucktail pattern that is quite effective on landlocked salmon, which are said to be genetically identical to sea-run salmon. So why wouldn't it work? After wading out and positioning myself as near to the heavy current as I dared, I made a series of quartering casts downstream and let the fly swing without stripping.

On my third cast I felt a heaviness, lifted the rod tip and braced myself for the frantic run and the graceful leaps of "His Majesty," which, of course, never came. It was fall; this fish was ready to spawn, and leaping into the air was the last thing on its mind. Instead it managed a couple of sluggish lunges, one or two slow, arduous, carp-like runs—more like walks than runs—and then burrowed into the current like a groundhog. A heavy fish, ten or twelve pounds, I estimated, he meandered one way, then the other, while I took line and gave line, all at a very leisurely pace, salmon fishing in slow motion.

In order to burn this historic moment into my memory—my first sea-run salmon—I looked up and beheld the underside of the abandoned railway trestle, Statler Tissue's unsightly backside and more debris on the opposite bank, the one we hadn't even tried to clean.

Meanwhile, my logy salmon was running out of steam. I had already decided that I was going to tail the fish, because—I'd seen the slide show—that was how you landed salmon. You lipped bass, netted trout and tailed salmon. Those were the rules. It turned out that tailing was not so easy. My hands are not large; the fish's tail was thick, wet and slippery. Even a dark, lethargic twelve-pound fish was too much for my grip. The final stage of the struggle resembled a rodeo event for kids. Finally, the hook simply fell out. The fish held in the shallows around my ankles until, fully recovered, he swam slowly off. That was enough for one afternoon. I waded ashore and never fished there again or had any desire to.

On the basis of that experience I decided that city fishing was not for me. Give me the real out-of-doors, the trees, hills and small, wild fish, and keep your inner city salmon. For years I never wet a line in downtown Augusta no matter how much I read about the "revitalization" of the river or the return of the striped bass, and no matter how many boats I saw as I drove to work. Then in '99 I traveled west with my friend Dan and had to reconsider my position.

Dan also works in Augusta in sight of the Kennebec, which he also does not fish for the same reasons that I don't. We have similar standards and for the most part enjoy the same sorts of fishing. We part ways on salmon (which he pursues in Canada) and, until very recently, bass, which, because Dan is a New Englander, he naturally disparages. Otherwise our tastes are much alike: we both prefer wading to floating, and the privacy of small streams to the crowds of larger, more famous waters, even if it means smaller fish, as it usually does.

One of our first stops out west was Poindexter Slough, a small spring creek that percolates through a lush meadow on the outskirts of Dillon,

Montana, before joining the celebrated Beaverhead. This was my third trip to the Slough, but Dan's first. I'd warned him in advance that this was not remote fishing. It was close to town. There was public access, a well-marked parking lot and heavily trod trails. The one blemish I might not have mentioned, because I barely remembered it, was Interstate 15, an elevated four-lane highway that actually crosses the Slough, but high above, barely noticeable. Also the train track that parallels the Slough—I might not have mentioned that either, because there's almost never a train. I always considered the Slough pastoral and serene, an oasis frequented by deer, ducks and wading birds. Beyond the highway the sage-covered hills stretch seemingly forever. And the stream itself—clear, sinuous, tranquil—is fertile and filled with vegetation and wild brown trout, some of which grow quite large.

But first we hit the local fly shop. Though we don't care for guided trips, we like free advice. The word was, not much was hatching on the Slough; stick with terrestrials. So we loaded up on hoppers and headed out. I was optimistic. No hatch was actually good news for me. On my first trip out, too much was hatching. One evening on the Slough I got caught in the middle of a veritable biological explosion. All sorts of bugs were hatching; fish were rising everywhere. It was like an entomology exam, and I flunked. Nothing, not a single hookup, not even a long-distance-release. Another time Tricos were hatching; that was almost as bad. I managed at least to catch a couple of small browns, but even in broad daylight Tricos are hard to tie on with shaking hands.

When Dan and I arrived, the parking lot was empty. Things were looking good. Then Dan decided that, despite my admonition, he would wade right out in the small spring creek, just as he might have waded a freestone stream in Maine. Poindexter Slough is slow and clear, more like a bonefish flat than a freestone stream. It does not tolerate being waded. I snuck downstream, about twenty yards ahead of Dan, and had a front-row seat for the parade of panicky trout. Trouble was, the fish spooked so far ahead of Dan that he couldn't see them, and he was skeptical of my reports. "Four fish just blasted past at about forty miles an hour."

"I didn't see them."

"That doesn't mean they don't exist."

Fishing partnerships either survive this sort of thing or they don't. Ours had endured almost thirty years of it. (Later he would have to tolerate an afternoon of my whining on a small stream in Idaho, because *I* wasn't catching fish.)

Dan continued trudging along, but was now at least trying to trudge more stealthily. Nonetheless, plumes of silt flowed from each boot. "See any more fish?" he asked.

"Can't see much of anything now. You're kicking up too much mud."

Soon, having proved to himself that his method did not work, he climbed out of the stream, and we moved off in separate directions. The stream curves and twists and folds back on itself such that it's possible to back away from one stretch and within a few paces hit more stream. After a while the terms "upstream" and "downstream" lose meaning. The willows and thickets along the banks hide the horizon (and the highway) and contribute to the sense of solitude and disorientation. After wandering around for a few hours, back and forth between sections, seeing no one, except occasionally Dan, I had a strange, exhilarating feeling of being surrounded by trout, some of which actually took my hopper. No lunkers, but several were a measured fifteen inches, strong fish and hard fighters.

Their first move would always be to the weeds; like rabbits diving into a briar patch, they'd plunge into the dense vegetation. I lost some, but a hopper can handle a heavy leader, and I hoisted a few out into the light of day, where they seemed shocked, almost embarrassed, that they, persnickety brown trout, had been fooled by such crude flies, big hoppers with rubber legs—like bass flies. What was the world coming to?

Dan, on the other hand, had been working diligently on the same pod of fish, determined that one would take. He tried fly after fly, but the

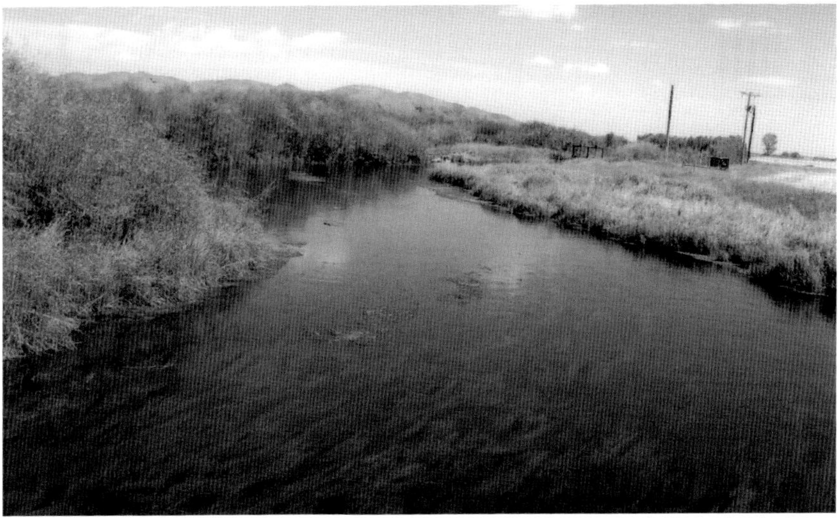

Poindexter Slough, Dillon, Montana—too urban for some, just right for others.

fish neither fled nor took. He even invited me to try, a sign of genuine desperation. I declined.

"If you've been watching them for that long," I said, "they've seen you." I caught my fish by casting blind to likely looking spots, spaces between the weeds. I suggested he try a different place, but he was determined to solve the riddle of those fish, and he wasn't interested in my opinion. New Englanders rarely take advice from Southerners on the subject of trout.

When we finally met back at the parking lot and compared notes, it turned out that I had caught maybe "half a dozen," and he had caught "a couple." Sometimes it's best not to be too precise, and sometimes, the best times, we actually lose track. For me this was such a day. Numbers aside, I was much happier than he, practically euphoric. Dan was ready for a beer. On the same day, under identical conditions, we had entirely different fishing experiences, but it wasn't until the end of the week that I realized just how different.

We were driving back to the airport, already reminiscing and rating the different waters. We agreed on our top-rated stream, the Lochsa. His second choice was that little stream in Idaho where he'd done well and I caught practically nothing. My second was Poindexter Slough. Rather than accept that tastes differ, we tried to settle the issue by arguing. I won; you'll have to take my word for it. I scored heavily and often. My best shot was, "Well, maybe if you found yourself in Chilly, Idaho, with time on your hands, that little stream *might* be worth fishing, but otherwise…" Maybe you have to have seen Chilly to appreciate what a devastating bon mot that was.

In fairness, Dan landed a couple of good shots too. In reference to Poindexter Slough, he said that the setting ruined the fishing experience. The stream was too close to town, too accessible, too civilized, too—of all things—urban. Worst of all was Interstate 15. He was fixated on that highway; those big rigs really bothered him. "It's just not like fishing in Montana," he said. "It's more like fishing in Augusta, Maine."

I was stunned, flabbergasted. I could not imagine two less similar places than Augusta and Dillon. The geography, climate, culture and, of course, the fishing could not have been more different. So what made him say it, other than to inflict pain and repay me for what I'd said about his second-favorite stream?

I've given the matter considerable thought, and my conclusion is that he did not like Poindexter Slough because the Slough did not like him. The Slough did not respond to his rough ways, his ram-the-fly-down-the-throat approach, his relentless efforts to pound that one pod of fish into submission. The Slough does not yield to force. It requires subterfuge and guile. Southerners may not know much about trout, but we wrote the book on subterfuge and guile (though naturally it's not called that). The Slough rejected his advances, so Dan resorted to name-calling. Augusta, Maine, indeed!

I am convinced that if he had caught what I caught, he would have loved the Slough as I did. As always, the secret lies in the fish. That is their power; they alter our perceptions. They alter not just how we feel, but also what we see and do not see. I saw a spring creek meandering through an idyllic green pasture, a Garden of Eden. Dan saw a big highway with a stingy little creek running under it.

His reaction and his comment made me reconsider my experience in Augusta years earlier. Suppose that dark, sluggish salmon had been a fresh, bright fish, just in from the estuary, its flanks still speckled with sea lice? Suppose it had tail-walked and somersaulted instead of wallowed? What if it had stripped line in furious reel-screeching bursts of speed? How would Augusta have looked then? Would it have seemed like the quaint New England town it once was, and still in some places resembles? Would the handsome, historic Fort Western on the other bank have been more noticeable than Statler Tissue? Would the church bells have tolled louder in my ears than did the traffic noises? Would the old buildings downtown have seemed quaint instead of just old? Would Augusta have glowed as luminously in my memory as Dillon, Montana, still does?

Too late to find out now. The Augusta dam has been removed, and the fishing action has moved upriver to Waterville. What a dump that place is. I think.

The Margaree, the Miramichi and Irving

I will never be a real Atlantic salmon fisherman, because Atlantic salmon fishing requires a different mindset from normal fishing. It takes a sort of Buddhist calm, an absorption in process, indifference to result and suspension of ego. Once briefly on the Miramichi I stumbled onto this mental state. It quickly dissipated, but I didn't miss it much or want it back. I prefer the caffeinated agitation of a hatch, a feeding frenzy; fresh water or salt, doesn't matter. Give me action or give me…golf.

I started Atlantic salmon fishing in Maine in the late 1970s with my friend Dan Onion. We fished practically every Downeast salmon river in the state—the Denny's, the Machias, the Penobscot, the Narraguagus and the Union—and neither of us ever caught a single fish. Not one. In 2000, Maine Atlantic salmon were placed on the Endangered Species list, which, if you asked me, was an improvement. In the late '70s, best I could tell, they were extinct.

For the next decade, I stuck to bass, trout and landlocked salmon, but Dan, when he did break away from work and family, snuck off to Canada, where he met people who had actually caught Atlantic salmon. In 1988 Dan said to me, "Let's go fish the Margaree."

"Where's that?"

"Nova Scotia. Cape Breton. It's beautiful."

"For Atlantic salmon? No."

"Jim, it's not like Maine. They actually have fish. And what else are you doing in October?"

He knew I hated not fishing in October. "I don't have the tackle," I said. "I don't have the flies."

"You can use mine," he said. "I've got an extra rod, and you can use my flies."

And so I capitulated and we went.

It was horrible. The water was frigid, my waders leaked, the river was crowded and its heavy current intimidating. My eight-weight rod was inadequate, and Dan's ten-weight loaner cast like a lead wand, heavy and lifeless. Dan caught three fish in four days, which for Atlantic salmon is fast fishing. Dan's catch rate could have ameliorated my misery, but it only made things worse: his unilateral success seemed the epitome of selfishness, never mind that he loaned me rod and flies, and let me fish each pool first. I still felt betrayed.

Also, the fish were dark and rather sluggish. The one faintly redeeming moment—comic relief—came on day two, when Dan hooked a huge salmon at a time when the guide was sleeping half a mile upriver. My trek to fetch and revive the guide and to convince him that Dan really had hooked a big fish (it is revealing when your own guide is incredulous), my efforts to help him hobble back downriver—his leg was still asleep—and the guide's attempts to herd Dan's fish by bombarding it with stones later became the stuff of, if not legend, at least amusing anecdote.

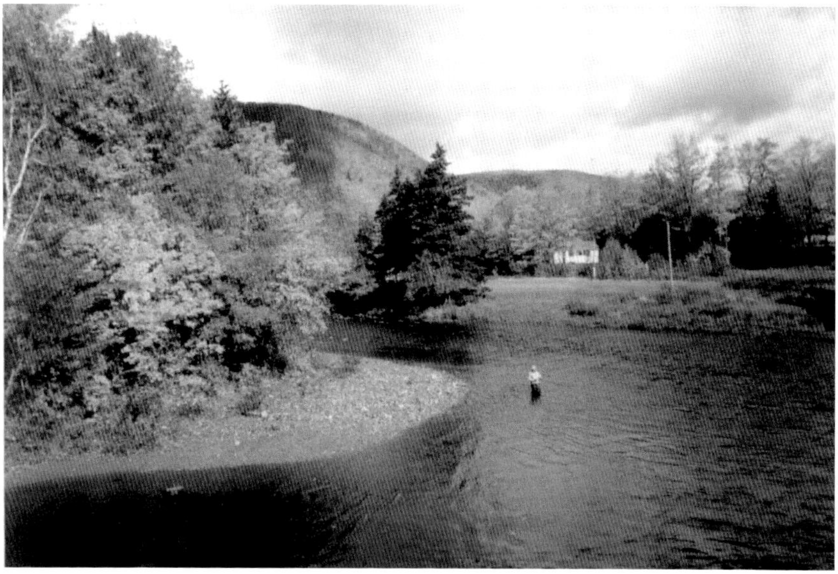

Dan Onion on the Maragaree River, Cape Breton Island, Nova Scotia.

Dan, on the Margaree, at the end of a rainbow.

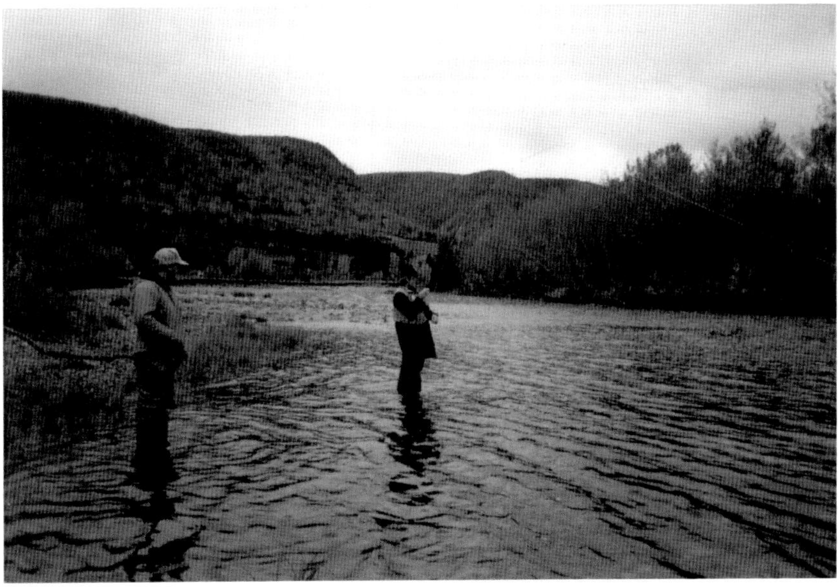

Dan, a few minutes later, hooked up.

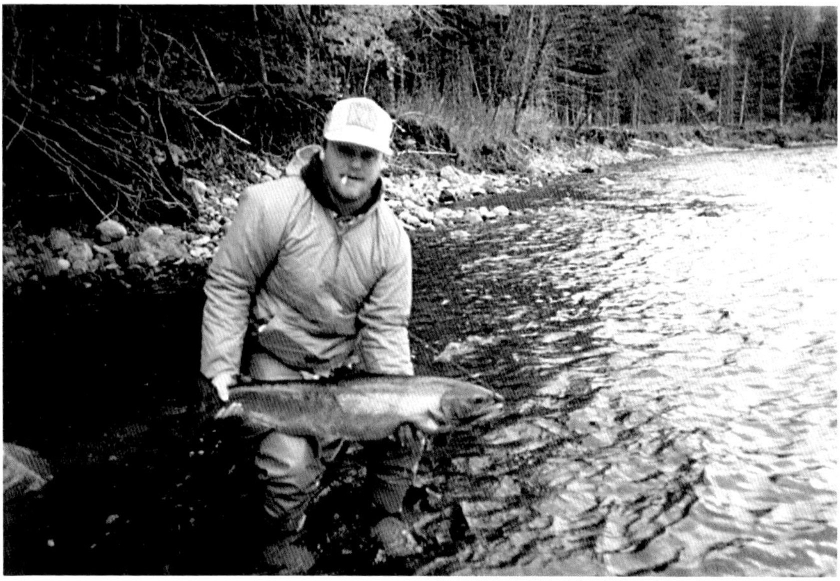

The guide with Dan's salmon.

"But don't take that to mean that I had fun or would *ever* want to do it again," I said.

Dan understood, and even though he made regular trips to Canada, and occasionally caught fish, he never wasted breath inviting me again until the summer of 2001, when he apparently figured that the statute of limitations on the Margaree fiasco had expired. Or maybe he expected pity.

That spring Dan had back surgery for a ruptured disc, had missed the summer fishing season and planned to make up for it in the fall. A cancellation at the Vickers Salmon Camps on the Miramichi in New Brunswick had left a vacancy in October. "It's Marty Vickers's place," Dan said. "He says there're fish."

Marty Vickers, a medical colleague of Dan's, had coached my son Preston in Little League—to a city championship!—*and* had fished with the legendary Ted Williams of Red Sox fame, who owned pools just upriver from the Vickers's place. A couple of very positive associations.

"You know," I said to Dan, "I still haven't fully recovered from the Margaree."

"This is different. It's a shorter drive and it's private water. We're lucky to get in. If there hadn't been a last-minute cancellation…"

"Okay, okay, I'll go."

"You will?" Dan sounded surprised.

"Yes, I will. I realize that I won't catch fish. I don't expect to catch fish. But I'm going to enjoy myself. And I am not going to suffer any more than is absolutely necessary. Those are my goals."

"Don't be so negative."

"'Negative'? I don't call that 'negative.' 'Negative' to me would be going to Canada, going anywhere, actually *expecting* to catch an Atlantic salmon." I was proud of my new attitude. Fish or no fish, I was going to have fun. Whereas Dan placed his hopes on the vagaries of a fickle, rare, almost extinct species.

The summer of 2001—such an innocent time! By October our world had been transformed, and not for the better. A former resident of Dan's, Dr. Fred Rimmele, had died aboard the plane that hit the second WTC tower. Dan was so hurt and angry that he tried to enlist. Dan is wiry and fit, but neither the air force nor the navy was looking for a fifty-nine-year-old doctor who was recovering from back surgery and post-op phlebitis. Dan was still on anticoagulants! The army, his last hope, hadn't given its final answer by the time we departed.

Neither of us considered canceling our fishing trip on account of 9/11. Fishing is important to us, a major part of our "pursuit of happiness," as guaranteed by the U.S. constitution, in the defense of which American soldiers over the years had fought and died, and would soon fight again. We had a duty not to let the bad guys deny us our constitutional rights. And that Dan, injured and no longer young, had volunteered to *be* one of those soldiers somehow gave us the right to go.

The Vickers's place is more like a home than a fishing lodge. Irving Vickers, Marty's cousin and our guide, is a rugged, medium-sized man with rheumatoid arthritis, which ended his logging career prematurely. Now he guides. As he greeted us in the backyard, Dan and I both noticed his gnarled hands and soft handshake. A firmer grip would cause pain.

Irving escorted us through the kitchen, where his wife Marsha was making cookies. He signed us in, and he sold us flies, then slowly led us to the river and showed us where to fish. The Vickers's pools occupy a short stretch of river, easily fishable in the low water. At the uppermost pool stands a warming hut and outhouse. We started in the lower end. After he pointed out the lies, Irving took a seat on a bench overlooking the pool. Irving is a not a guide who hovers over your shoulder critiquing each cast and fly. But neither does he fall asleep on the job. He functions as supervisor of fishing, an overseer. He treated us like adults. Fishing beneath his gaze, one senses a benign and wise presence. Irving is on his bench, and all is right with the world, at least with our small, protected slice of it.

The afternoon was sunny and warm; the current was amicable. The surrounding hillsides were pine, dotted with pale yellow poplar against an exceedingly blue sky. Up and down both sides of the river, at respectable intervals, fly fishermen stood waist deep casting repeatedly, or pausing to straighten leader or change flies. It was a very peaceful tableau, and soon the bombing in Afghanistan seemed far away. There will always be wars. Apparently, for obscure but deeply seated reasons, some men need to fight, but other men, for equally obscure, but equally deep-seated reasons, need to fish.

Occasionally a salmon broached, fracturing the calm and sending a ripple of hope and urgency up and down the river. And then the urgency dissolved and tranquility, the essence of salmon fishing if you let it be, returned. Soon the sun set, the air cooled and in lightweight waders I started to shiver. As if anticipating my every need, Irving built a roaring fire of brush and driftwood on the riverbank. Irving, who makes fire and does not criticize, was quickly becoming my favorite guide ever. I reeled in and walked over to warm myself beside the flames. I watched Dan cast until the last ray of light was gone.

At dinner we kept the TV off and talked of fishing, not war. It had been a slow season on the Miramichi due to low water. Dan seemed surprised and disappointed, but I was neither. I'd assumed that, for one reason or another, the fishing would be slow. Salmon fishing is always slow. That's how I like it; slow fishing levels the playing field. I was catching as many as anyone; I could pretend that the condition of the river was all that stood between me and success.

The next morning, bundled, warm and well fed, I took to the river and once again fell into the easy, hypnotic rhythm of casting. War and fish were equidistant from my mind. Casting was all. The sun rose higher; the air warmed, and at mid-morning I meandered back to the lodge for more coffee. As I passed Dan, who was casting intently toward a rock, he cut me a look. "Giving up already?" he asked. I smiled serenely. I know that real salmon fishermen do not take mid-morning breaks. They fish diligently from dawn to dark. So? I am not a real salmon fisherman. Nor am I meant to be.

After coffee, a homemade chocolate chip cookie and a nice chat with Marsha, I moseyed back to the river and resumed casting. Before I knew it, lunchtime had arrived, and after lunch I felt drowsy so I lay down to "read." Even Dan lay down, but he was restless and uneasy, because he's a New Englander, and he was neglecting his duty. Soon the Puritan guilt clicked in, and in a bustle of waders and boots, Dan was up and off to the river. "I'm right behind you," I said groggily. I am not a New Englander.

When I awakened, it was nearly four o'clock, and the sun was low. I donned waders and returned to the river. Dan had no luck, and his casting shoulder hurt. "I have some ibuprofen in the room," I said.

"I've got oxycodone in the car," he replied curtly. Oxycodone is a narcotic; he one-upped me on analgesics too.

My shoulder felt fresh and rested, and why shouldn't it? It had barely been used. But that evening I felt as if I cast with unusual grace and efficiency. I had a good rod and had discovered a new way of handling a long line that eliminated most of the retrieve and all the false casts: at the end of the drift, I let the weight of the water on the line load the rod, and then with a single haul I lifted forty-five feet or so of line and shot it back out to a new lie, without a single false cast. It was fun and, all in all, a very successful afternoon. By dinnertime I was rather pleased with myself. In my mind I was becoming quite the salmon fisherman—minus the salmon, of course. But what did fish have to do with it? They were merely an excuse to polish my casting and to pass a pleasant evening among friends. Soon it was time for bed.

The next morning, our last, dawned sunny, still and mild. I ate well and cast well—diligently and without hope, but also without despair. I fished the head of the uppermost pool. Dan covered the tail-out of the same pool. Irving sat vigilantly on the bench behind us. By 10:00 a.m. I needed a break. I approached Irving, leaned my rod against the bench and handed him my fishing vest. "I have to use the outhouse," I told him. "While I'm away, I would like for you to select a fly, tie it on and when I return, tell me where to cast it in order to catch a salmon." It was the first time I had directly asked for his help.

He nodded as if this were a normal request and smiled faintly, as if to say, "What took you so long?" As I headed to the outhouse, his arthritic hands had already begun sorting through my limited supply of salmon flies, and I had the feeling that he had been preparing himself for this moment all along. As perhaps, unwittingly, had I.

It did not occur to me at the time—because I was neither thinking nor analyzing—but later I realized that my handing over the vest and rod to Irving was the symbolic surrender of ego and the recognition of a higher power—Irving—that readied me for the fish. The outhouse visit was perhaps the final rite of purification.

On my return, my rod awaited me. Irving had tied on a rather unimpressive small yellow fly called a Squirrel Tail, not a fly I would have chosen myself, but that, I suppose, was the point. "All right," I said. "And where should I cast it?"

"At the dimple," he said, gesturing with his deformed index finger to a surface irregularity above a submerged boulder.

I nodded and marched obediently off to the river; never mind that I'd already made a dozen casts to the same spot during the course of the morning. But as they say, we never enter the same river twice, and certainly not with a fly personally selected and attached by Irving Vickers. On my second cast, a salmon came from behind the rock that formed the dimple and took my fly. Just like that, as if a salmon taking a fly was the most ordinary thing in the world, as perhaps sometimes it is.

It was a grilse, a small fish of about five pounds, but full of life. It jumped six times. While I played the fish, Dan came and stood beside me and made belittling comments. "Kind of small, isn't he?" I had to smile. He sounded so much like me on the Margaree. It *hurts* when we go fishless and our partner hooks up, particularly when the partner appears not to have paid his dues, not to have put in his hours on the river or to

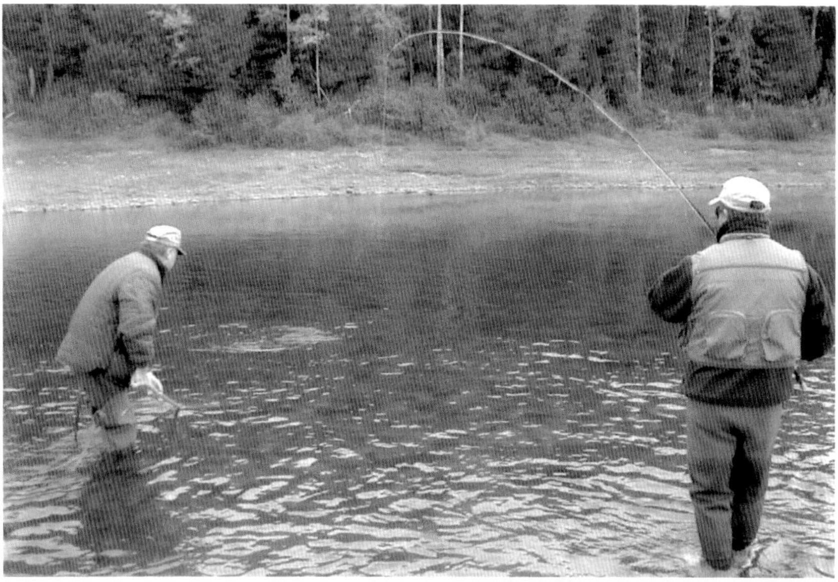

Miramichi Guide Irving Vickers about to net a grilse.

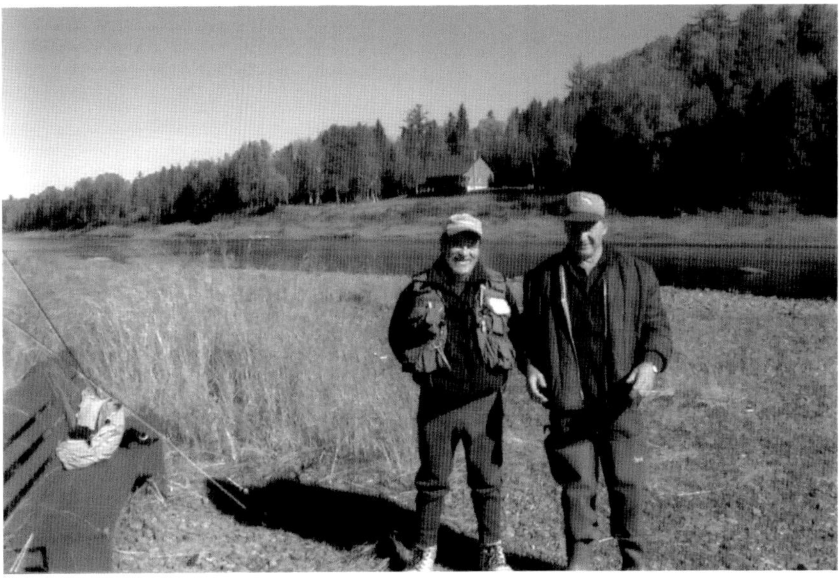

The author posing as a salmon fisherman beside his guide, Irving Vickers.

have suffered sufficiently. Dan no doubt felt that I had not *earned* that fish, though I certainly didn't feel that way. I paid my dues on the Margaree, and from my suffering I have learned an important lesson—*not* to pay any more dues. Enjoy the trip for the trip or don't go.

Dan, a gentleman, soon recovered his composure, congratulated me and even photographed my fish—the fight, a jump, Irving netting the fish and later, me holding the now dead fish by its tail. Irving wanted to keep the fish for his "winter larder," and this is his river and these are his fish. It was not for me to impose my catch-and-release ethic on Irving. I had not come to teach but to learn, and now, of course, Irving's authority was more unassailable than ever.

When Dan heard how it was that I came to catch the fish, he immediately attempted to duplicate the feat—the removal of the vest, the instructions to Irving, even the trip to the outhouse—but, of course, it did not work. It could not work; it was premeditated. Dan was merely emulating my behavior, without having entered the frame of mind that created it—the days, no the *years*, of mental preparation. Dan wanted a fish too desperately and was doomed from the get-go.

I sat beside my mentor Irving and watched from the bench, savoring the moment, consolidating the lessons of my unexpected success: you cannot take Atlantic by force; you must let the fish come to you in the fullness of time.

I felt badly for Dan as he made futile cast after futile cast. Finally I gave Irving a knowing little nudge with my elbow. "There're no shortcuts to enlightenment, eh, Irving?"

Irving, always the enigma, pretended not to grasp my meaning.

Atlantic Salmon Fishing—The Sequel

As we were riding back from the Miramichi, Dan broke the news that he had entered my name in the Cascapedia salmon lottery for 2002.

"You did *what*?"

"I entered your name in the lottery. I've been doing it for years, but this year they changed the rules. Now the permits aren't transferable. So if you win, you *have* to go."

"I don't have to do anything." I couldn't believe he would be so presumptuous. On second thought, I could believe it. Dan is a salmon fisherman.

"Jim, the Cascapedia is great water, much better than the Miramichi. If you can catch fish in the Miramichi, you'll clean up on the Cascapedia."

He knew I was in a good mood because I had caught the grilse earlier that day, the only fish of the trip. Now he was using it as a weapon. He expounded on my "salmon catching prowess."

"That fish was the proverbial exception that proves the rule," I said.

"I don't think so," he said. "I think you've got the talent."

"So what other names did you enter?"

"Just yours and Scott's. People I thought I could persuade."

Scott was a minister, a man of God. He was probably accustomed to being used.

"That's your idea of friendship, huh?"

"It's only for two days, Jim. I knew better than to press my luck."

If I was so appalled, why was I smiling? Well, for one thing, because Dan clearly knew the parameters of our friendship: any more than two days, and I simply would have refused. But two days? Somewhere over the last thirty years, Dan had earned the right to take our friendship for granted. I could not count the holiday meals I'd enjoyed at his house. Not to mention the fishing we had done together. We both fish with others, but more often than not, we fish together. We even have joint custody of a small boat. No fishing partnership is perfect, but over time you accept each other's imperfections or find new partners. Some differences you never settle, such as my fondness for bass, or Dan's for small brook trout, but on a scale of things, his presumptuousness was a peccadillo.

In February I got an excited phone call from Dan. "You won, Jim! You won the lottery!"

"I didn't enter the lottery." The salmon trip had slipped my mind.

"You got *incredible* water on the Cascapedia!" he said. "I've been trying to get on that water for years, and you got it! Wade-fishing the upper river. We don't even need a guide."

Then it all came back. "And what water did you get?"

"Oh, some crummy water downriver. Scott too. Downriver. Nowhere near as good as yours."

"Still my beating heart."

"Jim, you *have* to go. Wait 'til I show you this water. You won't believe it. It is prime water in one of the premier rivers in Canada."

Silence.

"You are going, aren't you, Jim?"

"Yeah, I think I will," I said. "But I'm not taking you. I'm taking Mike LaCombe. I want to go with someone I can trust."

For a moment he thought I was serious.

In June we set off for the Gaspe Peninsula, a lovely part of the world I had never seen before. We made a brief side trip to Prestile Stream in Aroostook County, one of Maine's few limestone streams, where we caught a few small brook trout. Dan was happy.

Rain greeted us on the Cascapedia; low clouds shrouded the surrounding mountains, dramatizing an already dramatic, ruthlessly logged landscape that reminded me of Montana, including clear-cuts. We stayed at the Relais de la Cache, a two-story white frame restaurant–inn–gas station situated more or less in the middle of nowhere, among a scattering of outbuildings, a burned camp, generator building, storage sheds and living quarters for the young couple who ran the place, Martin Gautier and his girlfriend, Adreanne, and their Shih Tzu Fred. Dan's reservations had been lost in translation, but there were no other guests. So the entire upstairs was ours.

Martin and Adreanne treated us like guests in their home. Fred regarded us as a source of food. The restaurant was a gathering place for locals and travelers, for loggers and fishing guides. Unfortunately, most of the conversation was in French, but the spirit of the camaraderie of isolation came through loud and clear. And we Americans were a welcomed diversion, and a captive audience, even if we couldn't understand the language. At mealtime Martin, dark haired and gregarious, would converse with us in English; Adreanne, less sure of her English, was quieter. Fred sat at our feet begging for handouts.

Bright and early the next morning, after a hearty breakfast, we hit the river. It was big water and, thanks to what Dan dubbed my "fabulous luck," we had a sizeable stretch to ourselves. In the first long pool, Dan hooked an eighteen-inch brook trout. Yesterday on Prestile Stream it would have been a trophy, but today, on big water and a ten-weight rod, the fish was a great disappointment. I took a photo anyway, and Dan pretended to be happy. We fished two other gorgeous and deserted pools without success. Then we broke for lunch, and after lunch we napped. Then it was back to the river, but it was not the same river.

In a matter of a few hours the Cascapedia had risen two feet and turned into café au lait. Entire trees, roots and all, floated past us. "I am not wading in that," I said. "You could get hit by a tree."

"That's not fishable," Dan said disconsolately. "How could that happen so fast? It didn't rain that much."

Frankly, I was relieved. Now we could do something else, something fun and, I was certain, catch exactly the same number of salmon.

We drove across the peninsula to the drainage of the lovely and less muddy Saint Anne River. On our way we stopped for a beer at the hotel. We hiked to a nearby overlook. Dan was still wrestling with the state of the Cascapedia. "How can a river rise so fast? There wasn't that much rain." Heavy logging had probably destroyed the buffer capacity of the hillsides. Later we had another lovely dinner with Martin, and Adreanne made a special pie. Then a slightly inebriated local serenaded us with guitar and vocals.

In the morning, the river was still unfishable. So we said our goodbyes, packed up and headed back to Maine. En route, Dan apologized for the fishing. He was very disappointed and, being the decent guy he is, he insisted on paying a large part of my bill, though that was not part of the arrangement.

"Don't worry about it," I said. "I had a good time. It was new country. And the Relais de la Cache was a hoot."

"Yeah, everything was fine except the fishing."

"You take salmon fishing too seriously."

"I caught a twenty-pounder there two years ago."

"And you let that fish ruin this trip."

"You're such a defeatist."

"Well, I'm not the one who's unhappy. You could learn from me. I didn't let last year's grilse ruin *this year's* trip. Because I understand that 'Atlantic salmon fishing' is a figure of speech. It isn't meant to be taken literally. For me, Atlantic salmon fishing is not about the fish. It's about spending quality time with your friends." I gave him a little pat on the back. "And it's about making new friends, and about seeing new country, that sort of thing."

"Sharing feelings," Dan, the classic taciturn New Englander, said with great irony.

"I don't know if I'd go quite that far…"

"Pat will like that. Next time I'll tell her, I'm not going fishing. I'm going off to share feelings with Jim."

"Well, the feeling I'd like to share right now is, next time Jim ain't going. Seriously. Do not enter my name in any more lotteries. I mean it."

"Don't worry. I don't think I'll be entering mine or anybody's for a while. This will about do it for me."

"Good," I said. "Now that we've got that cleared up, let's talk about bass. What's your problem with smallmouth bass? They're plentiful, they take flies, they jump high, they fight hard—what more do you *want* from a fish?"

With that Dan reached over and flicked the CD player on so loud that it drowned out any possibility of conversation. Ella Fitzgerald. We both liked Ella.

Wally

Wally is a bass fisherman who lives across from me on Lovejoy Pond in central Maine. Wally is a summer person. I am a year-round resident. Wally fishes lures from a bass boat with a big engine. I cast flies from a canoe. In other words, we have almost nothing in common except the fish. We both like bass.

At our annual lake association meetings we usually talked fishing, mostly his fishing, but one year he asked, "Why don't I ever see you out here on the lake?"

"I don't fish it in July and August," I said. "Too many big boats and jet skis for me."

"I know what you mean."

"I fish here in the spring and fall."

He looked puzzled. "So what do you do in the meantime, quit fishing?"

"Not entirely," I said, uneasily. I didn't know him well enough to tell him where I fished. That's personal.

"So where do you fish?"

I hemmed and hawed. "Different places, here and there." I nodded in the general direction of Rangeley. I didn't mention Morse Pond. I liked Wally. He was a nice guy, but I had my own fishing friends, fly fishermen, and Wally was the sort of guy we sometimes made fun of: he was thick through the middle, wore funny hats and fished from a big boat, with a bait casting rod. My fly-fishing friends and I had our standards.

This verbal thrusting and parrying went on for several years. Then in '95 I spilled the beans. That year the meeting was at my place; I was more relaxed than usual, and Wally had built a fly rod over the winter!

"A fly rod? Really?" I was amazed.

"I do a little fly-fishing at home. I told you that."

"Must've slipped my mind."

"But usually for trout, not bass," he added.

He lived in Pennsylvania, so they were probably stocked trout. Just the same, he had said the magic word, "fly-fish," and he immediately became more socially acceptable in my eyes. Next thing I knew, I heard myself blurting out, "Maybe you should come with me to Morse Pond sometime."

Wally's whole demeanor changed; he became silent and attentive. "Where's that?"

"Not far from here. Good fly-fishing for bass."

"You say when."

"I'll give you a call."

Next morning I sat bolt upright in bed. "What have I done?" I had invited a "summah person" into my sanctum sanctorum. What was I *thinking*?

I have a canoe stashed on Morse, which is a shallow, weedy, L-shaped pond of less than a hundred acres. A single meadow leads down to the otherwise wooded shoreline. A farmhouse sits high on a distant hill. There are no other houses in sight, not a single camp, and I have never seen a motorized craft on Morse. It is a sanctuary and insect factory, and it's loaded with bass.

Wally and I went one quiet August evening, and no fish were jumping. I wasn't worried.

"So how should I do this?" Wally asked from the bow. I paddled.

"Just put that popper along the edge of the weeds," I said. "The fish will do the rest." And they did, in a series of emphatic takes—deep swirls, explosions and even an occasional subtle, trout-like sip. By actual count in a couple of hours, we caught thirteen fish up to seventeen inches, which made for an average night on Morse Pond.

Wally said, "That's the best fly-fishing for bass that I have ever had!"

"I was afraid of that," I said, only half joking.

It was not the best night that I had ever had. Wally was too large for Morse Pond, literally and figuratively. He overpowered it, and he wasn't the easiest person to paddle around. Also, he was a science teacher, and quite knowledgeable about nature, and he shared that knowledge most willingly, sometimes too willingly. He taught as he fished. Were I a better student I would be able recite the names of all the constellations in the western sky.

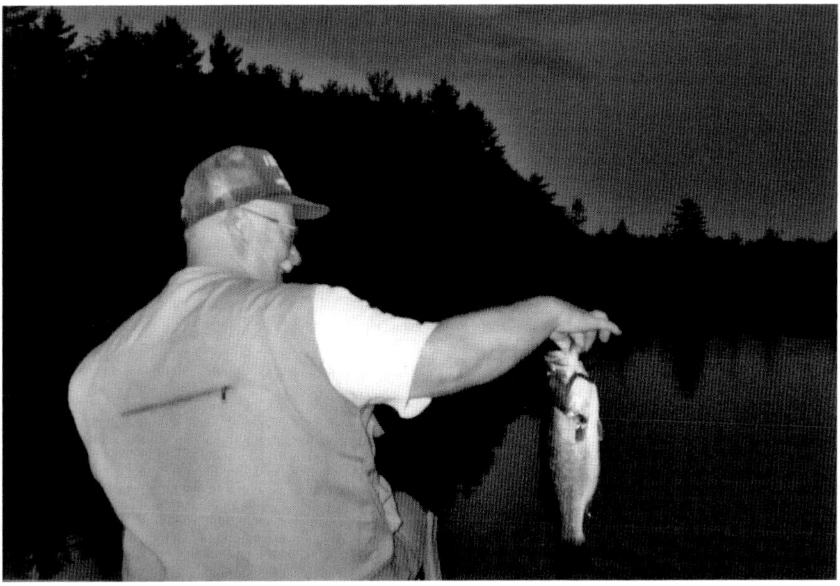

Wally Penrod on Morse Pond.

The next year at our annual meeting, when he asked when we were going into Morse Pond, I was evasive, and he was too polite to force the issue. He did give me his new phone number, but I didn't use his number that year, or the next, or even the one after that. I continued fishing Morse alone or with my fly-fishing buddies, but I had to admit that I was getting a bit irritated by the patronizing attitude that my fly-fishing friends took toward bass. Three of the four I had taken into Morse Pond (and the fourth no longer fished) had made comments either condescending or downright insulting. More time passed. Wally retired. Then he had a coronary bypass, from which he seemed to recover okay. One evening not long ago, I was fishing Morse alone when, paddling back, I saw someone with a fly rod walking along edge of the pond. Periodically he would take a few tentative steps into the water, sink in the muck and scramble back to shore. Someone was trying to *wade-fish* Morse Pond! What an idiot! I thought. But what a *determined* idiot. I secured the canoe and trudged back to my car, parked beside which was a big, familiar truck with Pennsylvania tags—Wally's truck. "Son of a gun!" I said. The same pond that my trout fishing friends sneered at, this poor guy wanted to fish so badly that a few months after his coronary bypass, he was trying to *wade*! The question then became, how do you tell someone that you have misjudged him and that you are sorry, without actually saying it?

The next day, I picked up the phone.

"You stupid SOB." I said. "You can *not* wade Morse Pond. It's soft bottom. You'll drown!"

He laughed. "So I found out." He was quiet for a minute. "That was you, huh? In the canoe?"

"Yeah, I didn't recognize you. And I thought you were a smarter man than that."

"Live and learn."

"So you want to try it from a canoe sometime? Or is that not challenging enough for you?"

"Just say when."

"Tomorrow, if it's calm. About five thirty?"

"I'll be there."

This time we both had fun. We didn't discuss the long hiatus between trips. We talked about the fish and the beauty of Morse Pond, and how lucky we were to have such a place where bass fed on the surface even in midsummer. Wally was more subdued than usual, and maybe I was too. I had learned a couple of things. Life is short, and enthusiasm counts for a lot. Fact was, Wally *loved* fishing for bass and he *loved* Morse Pond. The rest really did not matter.

"You'll have to come in here with me next June," I said, "when the fish are taking dragonflies out of the air. It's quite a sight."

"If you insist," he said.

"I do insist," I said.

And come next June I shall.

My Time among the Mainers

I never realized just what a peculiar people Mainers were until I learned about their fishing superstitions. According to their beliefs, there are only three "game" fish in Maine: trout, salmon and togue, known elsewhere as lake trout. All other fish, such as bass, pike, pickerel and perch, are "rough" fish. Apparently it is perfectly all right to catch "rough" fish for food, just so long as you don't pretend there's any pleasure to be had in the actual catching.

In 1975, when I moved here, I taught myself to fly-fish for the practically sacred brook trout. Amazingly, I actually caught some, thereby discovering one secret of brook trout's popularity: they're so easy to catch that even a Southerner could do it. Another key to their popularity is that they're delicious. An aggressive delicacy—a death sentence for a fish. Most Mainers, I was quick to learn, regarded brookies as "middlin' fodder"—food. No wonder the native fish are in trouble, especially in Maine's fragile streams, almost all of which flow over granite bedrock, the stingiest possible source of nutrients. New to the sport, I had no idea how much damage a single fisherman could inflict on a trout stream while staying within the law, but each year I found myself fishing harder and driving farther for fewer and smaller trout. Since the price of gas was rising, I decided to explore other options. I decided to try bass.

Central Maine is dotted with lakes and ponds, which I had scrupulously ignored in favor of trout streams. As my Southern fishing was exclusively in salt water, I knew nothing about bass, but I bought some popping bugs and one sunny, still, late-September afternoon in 1980, I decided to go, not fishing, but canoeing on North Pond, with my then-wife and nonfishing four-year-old son. The fly rod was almost an afterthought.

The pond was flat, calm and empty. Not a single other boat spoiled the tranquility and solitude. From shore came the sad sounds of hammering, camps being closed for winter, sounds that lent poignancy to the warmth of the sun. Winters hung like a sword over Maine summers, though lately that has been changing.

We paddled slowly along, my son's hand dangling lazily overboard. An osprey circled overhead. We meandered on until, several hundred feet ahead, there was a faint, barely perceptible disturbance of the surface. Circles dotted the water as if from a light rain, but there wasn't a cloud in the sky. It appeared that fish were feeding. The rise forms were so subtle—not a swirl among them—that I was certain they came from perch or sunfish. "I'll make a cast anyway," I said.

I worked out line and made a perfunctory cast with a small white popper toward the nearest dimple. For a few moments, nothing happened. Then in the clear water beneath my little popper, a gaping mouth appeared, a maw. It rose slowly, then faster, then like a football thrown through a plate-glass window. An enormous smallmouth bass shattered the surface, snatched my popper, rose several feet into the air and with a violent shake of its huge head sent my little popping bug flying back at me. The fish fell back into the water with a heavy splash, and the lake was calm again. The hammering from the camps continued just as if nothing out of the ordinary had happened, but I knew that my fishing life would never be the same.

That winter I bought bass fishing books, survey maps of central Maine ponds and more popping bugs of all sizes, shapes and colors, and come spring, I went exploring with my fly rod. I discovered that in late May virtually every rocky shoreline held smallmouth bass, and that often the fish were feisty and aggressive, assaulting a popper, but that other times they were remarkably trout-like and would sip mayflies from the surface as daintily as any brookie, and sometimes as selectively.

Once a smallmouth holding beneath a log fed actively on mayfly duns carried by a light breeze, but would not take my small popper. I had no mayfly duns, but I did have a Gold-Ribbed Hare's Ear nymph, which the bass took on the first cast. I was proud of myself for figuring it out and proud of the fish for its trout-like selectivity, though nowadays I'd never "compliment" a bass by likening it to a trout, or to any other species. It might even be the other way around.

It was when I first tried to spread the gospel of bass to my trout fishing friends that I ran up against the New Englanders' attitude toward

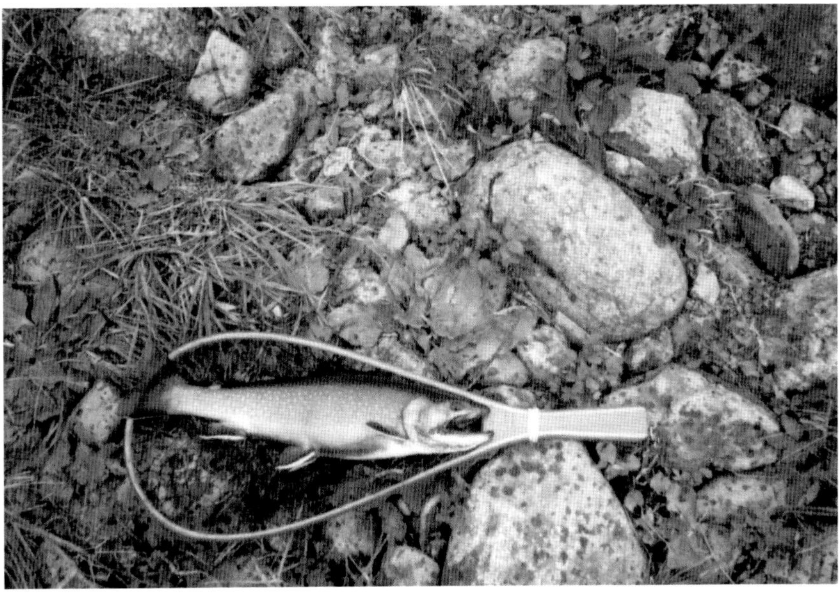

A Maine brook trout, a "game" fish, as opposed to a "rough" fish.

non-salmonids. One Maine writer has said repeatedly in print that he would rather mow his lawn than fish for bass—this from a man who *trolls* for salmon.

Assuming that this benighted New England attitude was correctible, I took my friend Dan bass fishing on Parker Pond. Parker is the most pristine and beautiful of all the local ponds, dotted with small, forested islands and lined with miles of rocky shoreline. It is a wonderful habitat for smallmouth bass. There is also a put-and-take salmon fishery, and immediately after ice-out, there is a trolling frenzy, but by late May the trollers have moved on, and Parker, in those days, would be pretty much deserted.

Dan and I took my canoe on a calm, overcast evening, and we caught over a dozen nice fish. Dan hooked and lost several before overcoming his trout-taught habit of a very light leader and a reluctance to actually *set* the hook, as opposed to the delicate lifting motion used for trout. (On the other hand, I've snapped off more than a few trout by giving them the bass treatment.) Eventually Dan hooked, fought and landed a respectable fifteen-inch specimen that jumped high and fought hard. "They are right spunky," he allowed condescendingly. Yet he gets ecstatic over eight-inch trout.

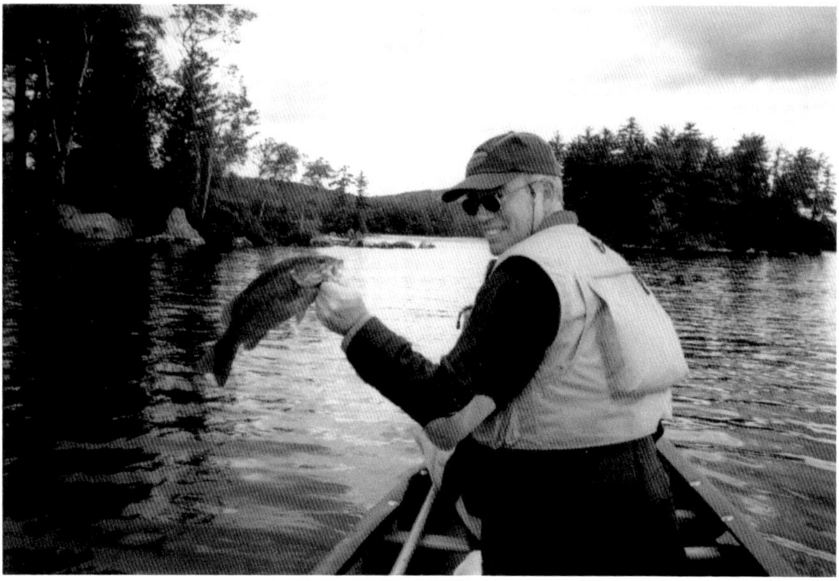

Ted Westlake on Parker Pond. Not all Maine fly fishermen ignore bass.

The problem, I believe, is that Mainers see brook trout as far more than a mere fish. Brookies evidently symbolize primitive New England, the wilderness that once was Maine, Thoreau country, and they apparently look at bass in much the way they regard other out-of-staters: if they aren't from around here, they cannot be worth much. It's not just bass either. Another trout fishing acquaintance of mine invariably referred to brown trout as "*German* browns," his tone of voice implying "foreign," and therefore "inferior." Never mind that brown trout are hardier and more selective than brookies, and they jump. They're also genuine trout, *Salmo trutta*, not char like the *Salvelinus fontinalis*. None of which makes a particle of differences to native Mainers, who take great pride in their prejudices.

After that experience on Parker Pond, Dan showed no further interest in bass fishing and I got out of the missionary business. I quit proselytizing on behalf of a fish that did not need it. I went fishing.

Unfortunately smallmouth did not solve all my fishing problems, because after spring spawning, they go deep. Actually, I'm not sure where they go, but they're no longer easily taken around the rocky shorelines with popping bugs, and I'm addicted to that surface action: the explosion of fish and water, or the more subtle swirl of dorsal fin, dark back, red eye—just so long as I can see it happen. Even a missed fish releases, in me, more adrenaline than a solid hookup sub-surface. It was time to switch species.

There's no record of exactly when largemouth bass were first introduced to Maine, but it was after smallmouth, which came in the 1860s. Now largemouth are widespread in central Maine. The beauty of largemouth bass—one beauty among many—is that they offer surface action all summer long. When brook trout sulk in spring holes and even smallmouth are elusive, most evenings largemouth lie in wait, under lily pads, beside boulders or beneath logs. In Maine, at least, they often feed on insects—damsel flies, dragonflies and even caddis. On certain ponds it is not *like* dry fly-fishing; it *is* dry fly-fishing, but the fish run larger, take more violently, jump higher and fight harder than brook trout.

Well, times have changed. More than twenty-five years later, bass are no longer a secret. In fact, it wasn't actually a secret before; there was always a Downeast smallmouth fishery in the Grand Lake area, but it was mostly anglers from out of state who enjoyed it. Now, in the new millennium, that too has changed. Bass are now one of the most

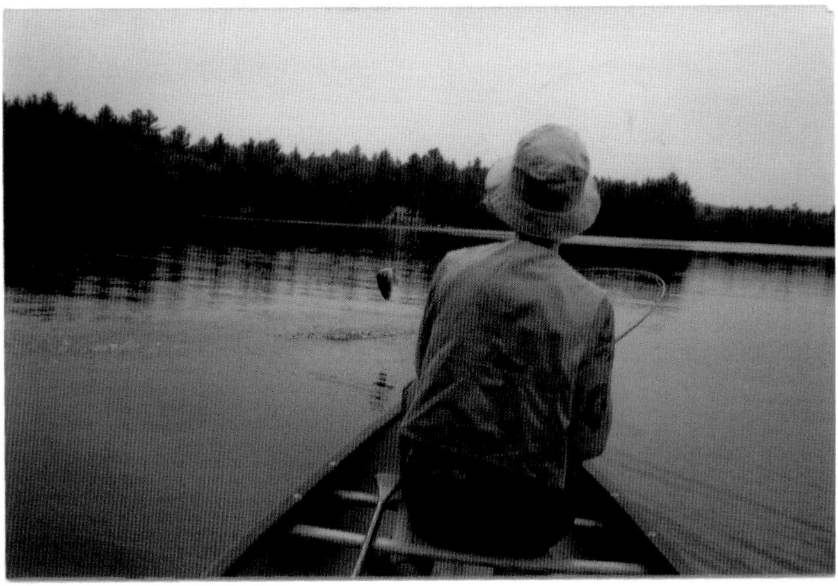

Cherie Wenzel hooks a nice smallmouth on Flying Pond.

popular fish in Maine, *even* among Mainers. Now even central Maine has bass fishing tournaments, and yes, the trout fishermen do snicker at the overpowered, sequined boats and the decal-covered jumpsuits. The irony is that in Maine the bass fishermen have done a better job of protecting their resource than the trout fishermen have theirs. Even though bass probably require less protection than trout, the bass fishermen have demanded—and gotten—not looser, but tighter restrictions on size, bag limits and fishing methods, the sort of regulations that, among trout fishermen, usually produce cries of "elitism" and "prejudice" against the age-old tradition of liberal limits and fishing with bait.

Bass fishing has even infiltrated Maine's bastion of hunting and fishing, its arbiter of outdoor taste, L.L. Bean. Its retail store in Freeport—a cathedral-like celebration of post-and-beam architecture, with richly burnished, laminated hardwood trusses, where antique fly rods and sepia-stained photos of days gone by are displayed like religious relics—is now well stocked with gaudy bass flies, fly rods and lines designed specifically for bass, as well as spinning rods and soft plastic bass lures. And there is no longer any stigma attached.

And, equally remarkable, in this new millennium, even my friend Dan now fishes for bass. A few years ago he bought a place on Parker Pond, and he has a grandson Sam, a fisherman, who enjoys catching bass and other "rough" fish from shore. Apparently if your grandson, a native Mainer, likes catching bass, it cannot be all bad. On the other hand, Dan insists on bass fishing with a seven-foot, four-weight fly rod, even though it's too flimsy to cast a popper and takes forever to land the poor fish. He considers it more "sporting," and that is the end of that. At least for now. Rome wasn't built in a day.

Pollock Rock

Most summers Dan Onion and I make a late season striper trip to the lower Kennebec. I never catch a striper, but I can hardly wait for the next trip.

I grew up catching stripers on the Chesapeake with spoons, buck-tails and cut soft crabs (and yes, briefly commercially, but that was when commercial fishermen were the good guys), but in twenty-eight years, I have never caught a striped bass in Maine. For much of that time, nobody caught them. The fish were gone, but now they're back. I've seen them myself, but sadly, not from a boat, but from my car as I was crossing the Fore River in South Portland. In the shallows, huge fish swirled and gulls dove, and there was not one boat to be seen as I passed helplessly overhead at fifty-five miles an hour.

The lower Kennebec's steep granite shoreline, wind-sculpted pines, extreme tides and heavy currents swirling through an intricate maze of waterways differ dramatically from the Chesapeake's sandy shallows and modest tides. Perhaps it is the clarity or depth of water or proximity of the Atlantic, but the lower Kennebec looks black. The Chesapeake's slightly milky shades of green fluctuate with the seasons, but the bay is never black. Both are beautiful, but the pastel shades of the Chesapeake, compared to the stark and harsher colors of the Kennebec, are somehow comforting, soothing. To me the lower Kennebec is intimidating, but not to Dan, because these are the waters of *his* youth. Though raised in Vermont, Dan summered in Maine. For Dan this is how an estuary ought to look; he is relaxed and comfortable here, because he is at home.

Dan keeps a seventeen-foot boat at Robinhood Marina between the Sheepscot and the Kennebec. We have a set routine: we shortcut through the Back River to the lower Kennebec and cruise the stretch from Phippsburg to Popham for signs of fish, but we never see signs of fish. So we pull into places where Dan has seen signs of fish before, or has even caught one—intriguing guts, runs and side chutes—and we blind-cast for stripers. Dan's uses a ten-weight with an enormous menhaden imitation, half a foot long. I cast smaller buck-tails and streamers, and then, for old time's sake, switch to a spinning rod and a Hopkins.

After we don't catch anything in one place, we move to another place where we don't catch anything. I never complain because I know that before we leave, we *will* catch fish, some kind of fish. Usually I am ready to move before Dan is, and I send a few nonverbal signals such as rubbing my shoulder, sore from casting, or even reeling in and "taking a break." Eventually Dan will reel in also. "Enough of that," he'll say. "I know a place we can catch fish."

We cruise downriver, past Fort Popham out of the mouth of the Kennebec into the open Atlantic. For me, accustomed to the relatively sheltered confines of the Chesapeake, entering the ocean imparts an eerie feeling. The next landfall is France. The boat seems very small. Unless it's calm, even Dan won't venture out, and even on calm days large groundswells, enormous mounds of ocean, roll in from beyond the horizon.

But between us and France lies a lump of exposed granite that we call Pollock Rock, and not far from Pollock Rock lies what we call Seal Rock, for obvious reasons. It's cluttered with these bright-eyed, curious creatures. The seals alone are adequate compensation for our efforts, but they're not why we came.

We cruise close to Pollock Rock and kill the engine. We put away our fly rods and switch to mackerel rigs, "Christmas trees," six jigs on a wire spreader. Six small pollock pull hard. And when they hit and you feel the weight, the reflex short-circuits the rational part of your brain that says, "Grownups shouldn't have so much fun catching small fish," and the impulse penetrates to a deeper, hunter-gatherer pleasure center. That fish weight feels good.

The excitement lasts until you actually see the six little fish, because until that moment, they could be *anything*, such as one large fish. You don't know. Small pollock are a beautiful shade of green burnished with gold. Sometimes we pull up small haddock, which are as sleek and bronze as sculpture. It's child's play, I suppose, but so what? And child's play on the edge of the ocean is a higher stakes game than, say, child's play on the Chesapeake. Anything can happen.

For instance, the last time out I caught half a pollock. The back half was gone, sliced cleanly off as if with a knife. "Look at that!" I said to Dan, who was struggling with fish of his own.

He glanced over. "Bluefish or shark," he said nonchalantly.

I guess the nonchalance came from his childhood, same as my awe came from mine. Sure the Chesapeake had bluefish, but the sharks were harmless dog sharks. A big one was two feet. But every once in a great while, a big bull shark would wander in from the ocean, tangle a gill net or seine and get its picture in the *Rappahannock Record.* Those occasional bull sharks were friendly reminders not to take the bay's benign nature for granted. The bay led to bigger things.

And now one of those bigger things had eaten the back half of my fish. After the shock of that subsided, the hunter-gatherer clicked back in. "Maybe I should take this half and put it on a bigger hook," I said.

"Might work," Dan said.

But I didn't get around to it, because I was having too much fun already. And the fun was just beginning. A few minutes later, I looked up and saw a school of fish chopping the water. A big school of fish. "Look! Are those blues?"

"I don't know, but whatever they are, I want them," Dan said.

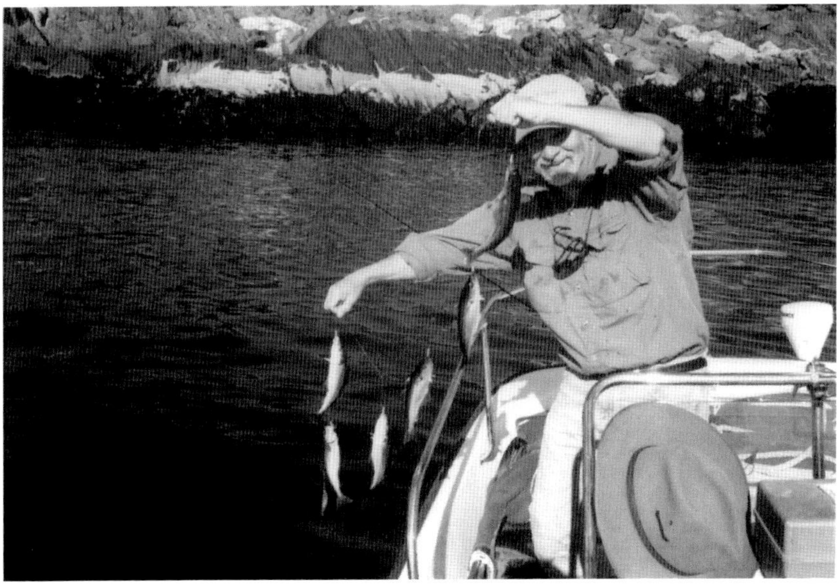

Six at a time from Pollock Rock (all released).

"You got wire leaders?"

But we didn't have time to change tackle, because the school was moving our way. When they got in range, I took a passing shot with my six-hook rig at the leading edge. Then a portion of the school passed under us; they were mackerel, not blues. Their variegated silver and black shapes *streaked* beneath us, streamlined and very fast. Then four hit my rig at once, never slowing. They were all about sixteen inches, maybe a pound or a little more, but at their speed they nearly removed the rod from my hand. "Whoa!" I said. Fortunately the drag was set very light and the line did not break. Then Dan was hooked up too. Four mackerel heading in different directions pulled even harder than six small pollock. It took so long to land those fish that we had only one other shot at the school before it disappeared, and we were losing daylight.

By then our arms were tired, our tackle was a tangled mess, our hands were nicked and scraped and our clothes smelled like fish. But we were happy, even if we had forgotten the original, ostensible, purpose of the trip: to catch striped bass on flies. Or maybe it was *because* we had forgotten the ostensible purpose and now remembered the *real* reason we had come: to catch fish, any fish, to cut our fingers, to tangle lines, to get excited and then to ride home, our hands perfumed with the sweet smell of fish.

To Nymph or Not to Nymph?

One rainy September morning, I arrived at the Kennebago River with my mountain bike to find that another fisherman with a mountain bike had pulled in just ahead of me. He looked to be in his late twenties, fit, not tall, with neatly trimmed hair. His fishing gear looked more expensive and older than his mountain bike. Simms waders, as I recall, and a Sage rod, decent reel, baseball cap, all well worn but in good repair. With tiny nymphs on his drying patch, he had all the earmarks of a serious fishermen.

As we unloaded and rigged up, we couldn't help but chat. Had I ever fished there before? he asked. I admitted that I had, but didn't tell him that I had fished it for twenty-five years and had hiked every inch of it.

"I've never fished up here before," he said.

Too bad for you, I thought.

I alternately slowed and hurried my preparations, because I wanted to be in front of him or behind him. I did not want to bike up the river with him, because I did not want him to know where I fished. Not that my water is so great, but it is good enough and it's *mine*, meaning few other people fish there, which is remarkable on a river as famous as the Kennebago. I'm as sociable as the next man, but I do not go fly-fishing to make new friends.

This fellow matched my pace step for step. When I sped up, he sped up. When I slowed, he slowed. So I could not avoid pedaling up the path, an abandoned rail bed, beside him. We continued chatting. He was a graduate student in marine biology at the University of Maine in Orono. His name was Tom, and he was from Missoula, Montana—the Bitterroot

Valley, one of my favorite places—which gave him immediate fly-fishing credibility. It also confirmed my suspicion that he could be a serious threat to my home water. But it turned out that next spring after graduation he was moving to California. "I like Maine," he said, "but my wife prefers the West Coast."

"That's understandable," I said.

We talked about fly-fishing in Maine. One thing led to another and the name of a prominent and controversial outdoor spokesperson in Maine came up. Said person had just returned from a Plum Creek–sponsored junket to Montana, and had written a glowing newspaper article about Plum Creek's land management, and how lucky Maine was to have such a responsible steward of the forests now operating in our state.

Which led Tom to ask, "Whose side is that guy on?"

I laughed. "That's a really good question," I said. Tom was pushing all the right buttons.

"At home, Plum Creek is considered the lowest of the low," Tom added.

I laughed again. "You have to understand," I said, "in his first life, this fellow was a Republican campaign manager."

"That explains a few things."

"Not long ago, believe it or not, he took up fly-fishing. Some of us thought it might improve his politics, but so far I haven't seen much change."

By then we had reached the point at which the tote road joined the main road beside the river. "Where were you planning on fishing?" I asked.

"I didn't have a plan. I never fished here before. Any recommendations?"

The moment of truth had arrived. "Were you telling the truth about moving to California next spring?"

He nodded. "I've already accepted a job."

"Because otherwise I might have to blindfold you."

"I doubt I'll ever fish this place again."

By this time I had mixed feelings about his departure. Maine needs more people like Tom.

We parked our bikes near a gravel pit, and I led Tom to an unmarked trail that led to an inauspicious-looking curved pool. Inauspicious to me, but consistently appealing to landlocked salmon now making their fall run. Tom stationed himself at the top of the pool, not the best spot. I fished the middle down with a streamer on a sink-tip line. Tom fished a small nymph beneath a strike indicator on a floating line. I kept an eye on him, because I was curious to see how someone from Missoula fished Maine waters. Turns out he fished them very well.

Fishing several different sections of *my* water, sometimes fishing behind me, he caught five fish to my one. I caught the largest, an eighteen-inch beauty, but otherwise Tom put on a nymphing clinic. He made it look easy, and, what was later even more remarkable, he made it look enjoyable. He had such rhythm: he'd cast upstream, follow the strike indicator down with his rod tip and, strike or no strike, twitch it at the end, just in case. Somehow the twitch turned into the beginning of his backcast, with which he repositioned his fly upstream—a smooth repetitive motion, interrupted at regular intervals by a quick lift of the rod tip, a take.

"I guess I'm going to have to get a little more serious about nymphing," I said when we were soaked by the steady rain and ready to quit.

"It can be a very effective technique," he said.

"I noticed." Occasionally I had fished with nymphs—a Tellico could be a killer on that river—but I fished them the same as I fished a streamer, down and across.

He deflected my compliments with his own. "You'd make a good Maine guide," he said.

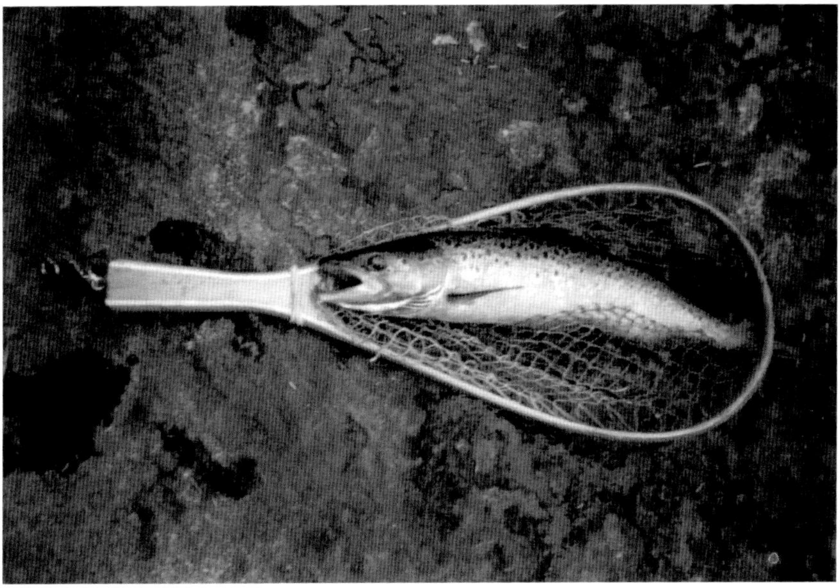

A landlocked salmon about to be returned to the Kennebago River.

I laughed. "Right. I got us lost on my *home* river."

"I wouldn't say 'lost.' We were just temporarily disoriented."

"I'll accept that." You can't really get lost on the Kennebago, because you are always between the road and the river, but I certainly had us wandering around for a while, breaking brush and crawling over dry-kill in search of a pool that is only three minutes from the road, though by the time we *finally* arrived, Tom probably thought it was in Canada.

True to his word, the next spring Tom moved to California, where no doubt the man is still catching fish. Untrue to my word, I did not take nymphing seriously. I gave it the same perfunctory effort as before; nymphing was a default solution, when all else failed.

Two falls later Dan Onion and I drifted the East Outlet of the Kennebec with a young guide we'll call Mark Evans. Small but wiry and strong, Mark is a native Mainer, following in and enlarging the footsteps of Dan Legere, John McLeod and Stuart Smith, who pioneered drift boat fishing on the East Outlet.

We met Mark early one mild October morning, dropped off his jeep at Indian Pond and returned to the dam to rig up and put in. Mark replaced my terminal tackle with a large stonefly nymph, a tiny trailing nymph and a strike indicator. He fixed Dan's the same and off we went. We anchored along the first big pool below the dam, and Mark showed us how to fish our nymphs. "No false casts," he said. "It's sort of an upstream heave, follow it down, then do it again. If that strike indicator goes under you set the hook. You may tick a few rocks, but that's better than missing strikes."

Working opposite sides of the boat, Dan and I attempted to follow Mark's instructions. Our techniques did not please Mark, or the fish. Lobbing these cumbersome rigs upriver wasn't much fun either. I never realized how much pleasure I took in the physical act of fly-casting until that pleasure was denied me. We drifted the upper river without hooking a single fish, though, according to Mark, we had each missed any number of takes. Dan and I had our doubts. In fairness, we were fishing behind two highly skilled bank-fishermen, also nymphing. We could see them hurrying along to hit the good pools ahead of us. I didn't blame them. I would have done exactly the same. My heart belongs to wade-fishing, as does Dan's, but his back had recently fallen into the hands of a neurosurgeon; hence the boat.

Mark did a great job with lunch—gourmet sandwiches, cheese and fruit—served streamside. Dan and I conferred over our meal and afterward we rebelled: we announced that we were going back to streamers. That was fine with Mark. Better to let us fail on our own than blame him. After lunch we were below the bank-fishermen, and after lunch we caught fish. Whether it was the streamers or the undisturbed water, we didn't know or care. Dan took the first from a deep, curved slot beneath a cedar tree. The fish leaped and did all the lovely things that landlocked salmon do. Mark netted and measured—seventeen inches—and then released.

Then I took a couple fish on streamers, and Dan got a couple more, and we were having so much fun that we invited Mark to fish, and he accepted our invitation. He used my rod rigged with a streamer, and his casts were something to behold. He covered water we couldn't reach, and he mended with a sharp, quick motion, much different from the lazy arc of my mends. He hooked a nice salmon too, which he lost at the boat.

"Damn!" he said. "That would have been the fish of the day!"

"Really?" I said. "It looked about like the others to me. Maybe a little smaller than my last one."

"No way!"

So we talked a little "trash." He was a top-notch trash talker too.

We hit Indian Pond at dusk; the air was still mild, the sunset gorgeous and all day we had been flanked by dark softwoods intermingled with blazing maple foliage. By the time we started home, it was night, moonless and very dark.

Route 15 from the East Outlet to Greenville is two lanes and featureless: no gas stations, no streetlights, virtually uninhabited. The road tunnels through a softwood forest of spruce and fir. Surrounded by blackness, the road conveys the claustrophobic feel of a coal mine. We rode slowly, scanning the road and right-of-way for moose, which are abundant in this area. Moose are dark and, unlike deer, their eyes do not reflect light. Every year in Maine a few people die in moose-car collisions. It had been too nice a day for that.

In fact, it had been a wonderful day. The weather cooperated, we caught fish and I learned a lot about casting, about mending and, most of all, about nymph fishing. Nymphing was taking over the fly-fishing world. Obviously the moral debate that had once raged in the literature—is nymphing actually fly-fishing or not?—had been resolved, or maybe just abandoned. These new fly fishermen appeared too busy catching fish to waste time debating. But what about the aesthetic argument? Was nymph fishing pleasing to the senses? Well, probably if you hooked up, it was. I wouldn't know. But what about the other 95 percent of the casts when you didn't hook up? And what about those—numerous to hear Mark tell it—missed takes?

When streamer fishing, I work close to my target. I see many more fish than I catch. I see at least half of the takes, and I see follows and swirls, flashes of green and silver beneath the fly. I might see a fish two or even three times before he finally takes. Each view of the fish, however brief and incomplete, sends a surge of adrenaline through my system. I'm energized. I know that fish are there, and they are interested. With nymphing, I lose the tactile pleasure of casting and the visual pleasures as well. And for what? More fish? That's not a sufficient reason.

"I don't think I'll ever be a real nymph fisherman," I said to Dan after a long stretch of silence.

"Me neither," Dan said.

"It's obviously effective, at least for some people. But for me it's not much fun."

"And every fish we took was on a streamer," Dan said.

"Yeah, but according to Mark we missed a bunch of takes."

"Yeah, according to Mark," Dan said. "Of course, he caught his, almost caught his, on a streamer too."

"The 'fish of the day.'"

"Right."

"You know, I used to think that saying, 'You can't teach an old dog new tricks' was a put-down of old people, but now I'm not so sure."

"Funny how that happens," Dan said.

"I think 'new trick' may just a euphemism for a fad or trend. People like us that have been around, we can see through these things."

"I couldn't agree more," Dan said.

We'd both turn sixty within the year. But sixty wasn't old. I didn't know exactly what "old" was, but it certainly wasn't sixty. "Old" was some indeterminate age beyond our horizon. "Old" was what happened to other people, mostly nonfishermen. "Old" was like that big moose that *might* have been lurking on the side of the road. If you were careful, kept a close lookout, took your time and didn't drive too fast for your headlights, you had nothing to worry about.

Measuring Success

Reviewing my fishing records for 1999–2000, I found four peaks of equal altitude: a bone fishing trip to Belize, dry fly-fishing in Idaho and, surprisingly, two bass fishing trips in Maine, one on nearby Morse Pond and the other on Lovejoy Pond, less than a hundred feet from my house!

These bass trips were not relegated to some subcategory of "best moments close to home." They were two of the four best moments, period. Which made me wonder, who in his right mind would compare bass fishing in Maine to trout fishing in Idaho, or bone fishing anywhere? But my records don't lie; the trips were four-star outings, and the narratives were feverish with excitement: "A magical hour on Lovejoy Pond!" "Incredible night on Morse…best number of good fish ever."

The fish on Lovejoy came on a calm September evening, after the summer people had departed with their high-powered boats and jet skis. I was sitting out back, barbecuing chicken, sipping a beer and gazing absentmindedly at the satiny surface of Lovejoy Pond. Such water is often described as "mirror" smooth, but the slick surface often functions like a window: it lets you see at least a little ways into the pond. A wind-ruffled lake is like a curtained window: even small waves conceal the lake's secrets. But now even the skittering water bugs were visible as a generalized busyness, background noise easily ignored. Then came a swirl, not the dimple of sunfish or perch, but a sizeable excavation, as if a dishpan of water had been scooped out, leaving ever so briefly a crater. I sat my beer down.

Soon there was another similar swirl, and I walked over to the water for a better look. The lake was carpeted with flying ants. From a hundred feet I hadn't seen them, because they were very small, barely moved and didn't break the surface tension, but were stuck to the water. Like flies to flypaper, they lay helplessly wriggling their legs and wings. Bass were mercilessly picking them off.

I keep an eight-weight rod rigged and ready for just such emergencies. Within minutes of spotting the first rise, I was in my canoe working out line. The fish were cruising. The trick—it's taken a few years to figure out—is to pick an individual fish, plot its course and put a small black popper in front. You have to lead the fish. Twitch the popper once and wait—sometimes a few minutes, sometimes not at all. As often as not, the next rise is in another direction.

That night, after a few miscues, I calculated correctly and connected. A big fish sipped my little popper with the same insouciance with which he was nibbling ants. There was a gratifying explosion of shock when I lifted the rod, and a very satisfying heaviness. This was a *good* fish. He burrowed toward the bottom, but in twenty feet of water there was nothing to wrap and no place to hide. So he came up, then down, then sideways; he pulled the canoe for a while. Then he came to hand, his mouth gaping as he tried to regurgitate stomach contents, in this instance a crayfish the size of a small lobster. It was a nice bass, a measured seventeen inches, but it was a *huge* crayfish, a trophy crayfish. I'd caught bass that size before, but I'd never seen a crayfish this large. I kept a broken-off claw as a souvenir; the fish got the rest, which was too large to regurgitate.

I revived the bass and he swam off, chagrined, I'm sure. That bass was not hungry. He had just engulfed a huge crayfish, which he hadn't even begun to digest, and yet here he was, twenty feet off the bottom, surface feeding on tiny flying ants. An acre of those ants wouldn't amount to the tail meat of that crayfish! Metabolically it made no sense. There was only one explanation: those ants were delicious. They were dessert, a delicacy. That a bass, a *fish*, was capable of such dietary indiscretions endeared him to me even further—as if *that* were necessary. Because I was thinking that after the barbecued chicken, I was having ice cream. Turned out, after fooling around with those fish until dark—I hooked five more!—ice cream was all I was having. That chicken was charcoal. Which seemed fair: I ruined the basses' meal; they ruined mine.

The largemouth on Morse came on another calm evening. The pond's surface was black and slick as obsidian until dusk, when caddis flies began to hatch. The bass were soon to follow, and these fish were not sipping. Their grenade-like takes shattered the calm. No sophisticated tactics or strategy required. Just cover the rise and hold tight to your rod. I like Morse for, in addition to its fish and insects, its solitude, but this night the presence of two other anglers sweetened my success, because they were bait casting in the same cove and catching nothing. Usually with bass, bait-casting is more effective; so on those rare occasions when the opposite is true, it is hard not to gloat. In Maine there's a dysfunctional relationship between fly fishermen and bass fishermen: bait casters often sneer at fly fishermen and most Maine fly fishermen often sneer at bass. That night I felt as if I'd I struck a blow for, and against, *both* sides.

Clearly factors other than size, number and species figure into fishing success. Aesthetics and context also count. A measure of fishing success more accurate than pounds or inches might be blood levels of endorphins or whatever chemicals are responsible for the fishing-induced euphoria that makes those glorious moments like mine on Morse and Lovejoy so incredibly, indelibly sweet. So what if this method of scorekeeping favors the more easily excitable? Retaining childlike enthusiasm for fishing is a gift. We should use it.

One sad fact is that these peaks can rarely be reproduced. Even if you repeat the experience—hard enough in its own right—the excitement will never be quite the same as that *first* time. Hence the need to find

A quiet evening on Morse Pond.

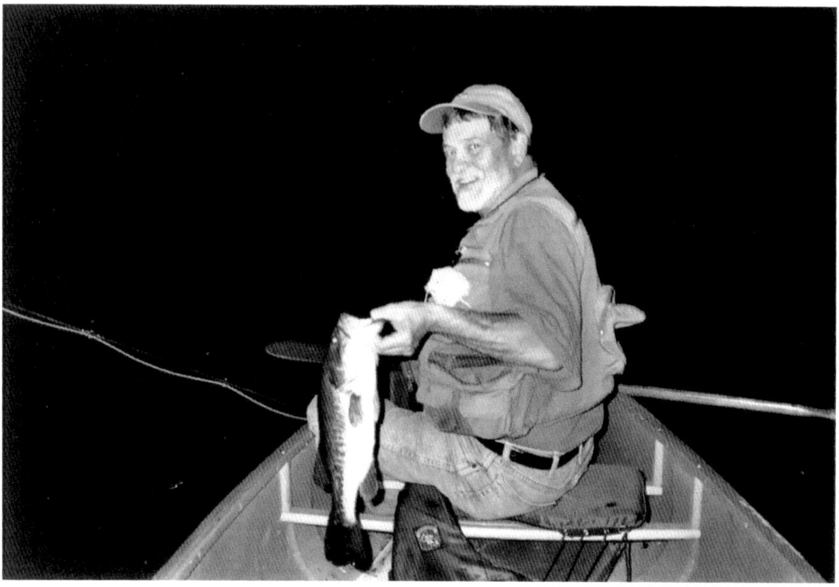

And later on Morse Pond.

new peaks, but that does not necessarily mean finding new territory, or traveling to exotic locales. For instance, in early summer, the largemouth bass on Morse Pond feed selectively on hovering dragonflies and damsel flies. A floating imitation will not work; a popper won't work. The fish want—they demand!—an airborne insect. The bass lie beneath lily pads and beside logs waiting in ambush, and at the precise moment large fish leap two or maybe three feet into the air for a bug. The fish are so absorbed in their feeding that you can canoe quite close to watch. As a spectator sport it is fascinating, but I wanted to participate. I wanted in.

I made a few unsuccessful efforts with an apparatus consisting of an extension pole and a fly suspended with one-pound test, but, aside from not working, it also looked ridiculous, and it would take at least three hands to operate successfully. So I have expanded the concept, enlarged the vision to one involving two canoes, two fishermen and a photographer. Imagine hooking an airborne fish and *capturing* it on film! That would be a peak among fishing peaks, the Mount Everest of Matching the Hatch. It's too late for this year, but I'm already making plans for next year's expedition. I'm assembling gear, lining up my team, plotting our assault on that loftiest of all summits and waiting impatiently for the snow to melt.

Assessing Failure

Well, as these things often happen, several years passed before I actually implemented my plan, several more years of frustration at my inability to solve the quandary of bass feeding on airborne insects. In 2004, I was ready.

The plan in its final conception was elegantly simple: two canoes, two fly fishermen, with the fly suspended between them, connected to one line with a spider web of one-pound tippet, to the other with serious leader material. When the bass took the fly, the light tippet would immediately break, leaving the other fisherman, me, to fight the fish.

The next step was assembling my team. I tried to convince my friend and master guide, Stuart Smith, that this might be an opportunity to make fly-fishing history, to enter his name into the annals of Maine fly-fishing lore alongside the likes of Carrie Stevens and FlyRod Crosby. He was not easily persuaded. Master guides rarely are. So I showed him a published article describing how the legendary Joe Brooks had once attempted a similar feat on the Madison with trout, which were feeding on airborne dragonflies. His fish were hard against a grassy bank. By attaching tiny treble hooks distal to his fly, he was able to snag the grass with the treble, leaving the fly to dangle alluringly above the feeding trout. He was said to have succeeded, but—important point—there was no photographic evidence.

"We could be the first to actually document it on film," I said one midwinter morning.

"I don't know, J.H.," he said. "Still sounds pretty wacky to me." Then he laughed.

I took that as a "yes."

Next we needed a photographer and someone to paddle the second canoe. My top candidate for photographer was Dr. Dean Bennett, professor emeritus of science education at the University of Maine at Farmington and author of such books as *Maine's Natural Heritage*, *The Allagash* and *The Wilderness from Chamberlain Farm*, among others, including a high-school text and popular series of children's books, all of which he illustrated with his own pen-and-ink drawings, watercolors and photographs. His photo credits include the only known unstaged photo of a Maine coyote chasing a deer—lucky, yes, but no gimmicks or digital trickery, just the coyote and buck both stretched out on a dead run. In the same book there's a stop-action photo of a ruby-throated hummingbird, its wings not the usual hummingbird blur, but frozen, each individual feather as distinct as a finger—taken with an elaborate custom-built strobe-flash-timer system Bennett had designed himself.

The only question was, was Bennett qualified?

Ultimately I decided that he was, not because of his education, his literary or artistic accomplishments, but on the basis of his less well-known, groundbreaking bowhunting movie, a work that set new standards for shakiness in cinematography. For nauseating, vertiginous viewing, it put *The Blair Witch Project* to shame. Bennett had cleverly mounted a camera to his bow so that the viewer could look along the hunter's line of sight at his target, in this case a snowshoe hare, or so Bennett claimed. Something blurry did indeed move in and out of the bouncing frame; it could have been a rabbit; it could have been a beach ball, though a rabbit seems more likely. The film lasted a mere ten minutes, though it seemed an eternity. Through it all, Bennett continued his narration with great solemnity—"Here we see the elusive, variable hare lurking in the underbrush"—as if anyone could actually discern anything. It was *just* the spirit I was looking for. Bennett was clearly the man for the job and, recognizing a career-making opportunity when he saw it, he signed on without a moment's hesitation. He even volunteered the services of his charming, intrepid wife and partner Dr. Sheila Bennett, professor of natural sciences, to paddle the second canoe. Our team was now complete.

We rendezvoused on a hot, sultry evening, July 1, 2004. Right away I spotted trouble. Bennett was lugging a heavy thirty-five-millimeter camera with a telephoto lens and a satchel of expensive-looking accessories. "How much is that stuff worth?" I asked. I could envision us rolling over and dumping everything in a moment of excitement.

He didn't know precisely what it was worth. "*Thousands*," he guessed.

"Is it insured?"

"Possibly, under my homeowners."

"I should've had you sign a release."

"Oh, don't worry about it, Jim."

"You all heard that," I said to the others.

So off we went with Dr. Dean paddling my canoe and Dr. Sheila paddling Stuart's. In the heat of the evening, not much was happening. To kill time and hone our skills, Stuart and I fished. What else was there to do? Casting along the lily pads and fallen trees, we caught nothing. Then it happened: Dean and I, in the lead canoe, came upon a bass holding beneath a log and feeding on airborne damsels. He was of average size, maybe a pound, but he was perfect for our experiment. Careful not to spook the fish, we backed away and summoned Stuart and Sheila. Before moving into position, I attached an iridescent blue damsel imitation—"darning needle," they're called—with eight-pound test to my tippet, and to the fly's thorax with a single strand of one-pound test I connected Stuart's line. We suspended the fly, just as we had rehearsed, moved our canoes into position and waited. Dean was poised and ready with his camera; Sheila steadied the second canoe to my left, while Stuart and I dangled the blue damsel fly imitation enticingly above the fish's lie. We made the little fly dance like a marionette, zip about and pirouette like a ballerina and then hover just above the log. Nothing. Evidently the commotion had disrupted the fish's rhythm. He sulked; or perhaps he'd moved off.

"How can he resist that?" I asked.

"I don't know," said Stuart.

"Maybe it's the fly," I said. "Yeah, it must be the fly." I was digging into my collection of damsels and dragonflies, looking for a slenderer version, when Stuart yelled, "Now! Now! Aw Jeesum, Jim! He tried for it." Even over Stuart's anguished cries, I heard the sickening sound of the fish splashing heavily back into the water.

"Did you get it, Dean?" I asked.

"Ahm, I was adjusting a setting."

"Aw, Jeesum, all that time!" Stuart said.

"It's okay, it's okay," I said. "He'll come back."

"He just couldn't quite reach it," Stuart said. "It was just a tiny bit too high."

"We'll hold it lower. We'll get him this time. You ready Dean?"

"Ahm, yes, I believe so." Evidently focus and lighting were more challenging than he'd anticipated.

We waited and waited, but of course, the fish never returned. No telling what he actually saw the first time he jumped, but whatever it was, we were busted. The jig was up, the sun was down and no other fish were jumping.

Disconsolately, we paddled back in the almost dark of the evening. To their everlasting credit, my three cohorts were upbeat and supportive. "Well, it did sort of work," Stuart said. "The fish *came* for the fly."

"It was a disaster," I said.

Sheila was her usual kind self—she saw the humor in it—and Dean was already making plans for a second attempt. "Next time I need to be on shore," he said. "I need to have the camera on a tripod."

"No, there's not gonna be a next time," I said. "That's it. I appreciate your patience and help—you're great sports—but that's it."

They did not argue too strenuously or too long.

In my imagination, that suspended damsel fly imitation drove fish wild, made them reckless and was so effective that Stuart and I would be able to fish it blind along promising logs and lily pads and *suck* fish out, as with a vacuum cleaner. They would be powerless to resist. If a suspended fly was just another marginally or intermittently successful fishing method—and logistically five times harder—why bother?

Well, at least we hadn't dumped Dean's expensive equipment overboard, and nobody got hurt or hooked on a backcast. Looked at that way, the evening wasn't a total failure. Now my curiosity was satisfied; no longer would I be unsettled by the sight of bass leaping into the air. I could sit back and enjoy it, and not wonder if I might be missing a great opportunity of matching that hatch. At least we performed the experiment; the *experiment* was a success. It's the fishing method that failed. Now I knew, and now I could move on.

And, anyway, we did get one good picture that night of Dr. Dean Bennett, professor emeritus, holding a nice bass—never mind who caught it—a photo taken, by the way, with my little point-and-shoot.

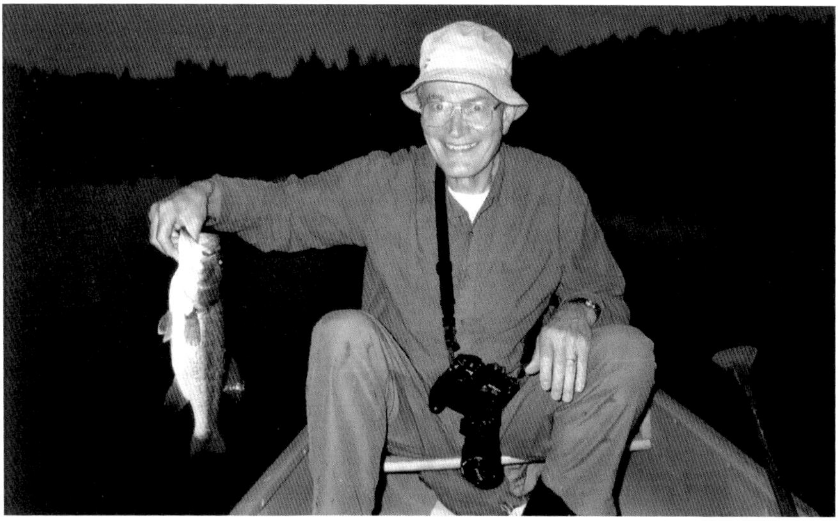

Dr. Dean Bennett with a healthy specimen from Morse Pond.

Reading Proust in Montana

Some people said it was reckless at my age to drive alone from Maine to Montana to fish. Others said I was foolish to attempt to read the complete works of Marcel Proust. So it seemed to me that Proust was a natural, if paradoxical, traveling companion to Montana. Or perhaps not so paradoxical: though Proust was a delicate city dweller, he worshipped nature and loved the "the fortifying thrill of solitude," two ingredients important to enjoyable fly-fishing.

Twenty-four hundred miles separate Wayne, Maine, from Big Timber, Montana, but by the end of day three I managed to be fishing the upper reaches of the Boulder River. I just wasn't enjoying it very much. In the twenty-three years since I'd first fished the Boulder, it had been discovered not only by fly fishermen, but also by religious groups, who'd built and posted summer camps along the river's banks. Believing that a trout stream was far more important to *my* religion—fly-fishing—than to theirs, I resented this intrusion. Yes, Montana's Stream Access Law guaranteed my right to fish in "their" river, but it did not guarantee I would enjoy it. Trespassing is more than laws and boundary lines; it is a state of mind.

So in the middle of a restless night spent in the back of my vehicle, I made a decision in favor of "the fortifying thrill of solitude," even if it meant, as it usually did, small fish. And in the morning I set out for the upper Ruby, not exactly virgin waters, but now time and memory worked in my favor: from my trip there in '82 I recalled posted land, difficult water and no fish. I had nowhere to go but up, figuratively and literally. In '82 I'd fished the lower river; this time I went upstream to where the river was a trickle and the road ran through public land until, on paper at least, both river and road dwindled into invisibility, leaving, one hoped, not even enough water for a baptism.

And there on the Ruby I found, for the moment, the Montana that I was seeking. For the record, the fish were *tiny* stocked grayling and hybrids, and no self-respecting fly fisherman would or should go there, except *perhaps* for the "scenery," and even that was rather bland—beige hills with but a single green stripe running crookedly down the middle. Montana offers many better places to fish and photograph, but for now, this one suited me fine.

I met a few other lost souls along the way, all fly fishermen, none of whom seemed to mind that the fish were tiny and the road terrible. They'd been fishing more famous places and had come here for a respite, a retreat from the competitive pressures of guided float trips, major hatches and big fish. Their occasional appearance provided pleasant company and made the contrasting solitude even more "fortifying."

If you are patient with a piece of water, any water, it will slowly reveal its secrets, the larger fish that even the smallest streams conceal. One day downriver I stumbled onto a Trico hatch in a shallow clear run, with snouts of sizeable browns rising among the matted rafts of tiny mayflies. Due to the clockwork regularity of the hatch and the benevolence of the fishing gods, over the next few days, through trial and error, and more errors and lucky guesswork, I was able to hook and even land a number of these browns. To see the rise, lift the rod and feel the resistance and to realize that from that dense myriad of flies, an armada of tiny duns, *mine* had been selected, the *chosen* one—well, the euphoria that follows, the sense of acceptance, would be as inexplicable to the nonfishermen as it would be self-evident to a fly fisherman.

That evening I wondered how Proust might have handled that glorious spectacle. *Could* he have handled it? Or would this vision of fish appearing miraculously in crystalline water to sip the most delicate, well-formed insects have overpowered his senses? Here is Proust beside still water:

> *The tiled roof cast upon the pond, translucent again in the sunlight, a dappled pink reflection which I had never observed before…I cried aloud in my enthusiasm…Gosh, gosh, gosh, gosh! But at the same time I felt that I was in duty bound not to content myself with these unilluminating words, but to endeavor to see more clearly into the sources of my rapture.*

Four "goshes," from a single change of light, and yet he probably could have handled more, because after the enthusiasm, perhaps even during it, came the analysis. His self-consciousness was always interposed between his eye and his emotions, protecting his delicate sensibilities like a shield. Though his entire being might have vibrated to the miracle of trout-on-Tricos, his hands would not likely have shaken as mine did. And as marvelous as he found nature, it was no match for the appeal of the mysteries of his own mind and heart. For that we can pity him, but at the same time be grateful that he kept such meticulous records of his explorations. There's nothing quite like it. Proust was the Lewis and Clark of introspection: as if pursuing the mysterious subterranean origin of a spring creek, he followed every rivulet of feeling and perception to its source.

For the next three weeks I followed many rivulets of my own until, saved from myself, my explorations were interrupted by a welcomed visit from the lovely Patricia, a blue-eyed blonde from back East. She is not a fly fisherman, but is omnivorously curious; so in her honor I had planned to demonstrate the glories of fly-fishing on the catch-and-release section of the Lochsa River, where the native cutthroat trout tend to be accommodating and beautiful. The plan worked perfectly, to a point.

The morning was warm and sunny and we located a beautiful crescent-shaped pool, its inside curve a sandy beach where Patricia could sit, enjoy the sunshine, the splendor of the surrounding mountains and her man fly-casting on the Lochsa's lovely emerald waters. And soon enough, her man hooked a beautifully marked twelve-inch trout, which he played, netted and held triumphantly for her to admire. Unfortunately, the hook-set had slightly torn the fish's jaw, from which a single drop of blood oozed.

"That looks painful," said Patricia.

Abashed—he had not expected her to side with the fish—her man quickly, unceremoniously released the wounded trout.

"And it was at that moment," Proust noted, when a passerby failed to appreciate that "dappled pink reflection" on the pond, "that I learned that identical emotions do not spring up simultaneously in the hearts of all men in accordance with a pre-established order."

In this instance, Patricia appreciated the dappled sunlight and even pointed out a swarm of tiny insects hovering over the water. It was the hooked fish and the drop of blood that unsettled her.

Soon her visit was over and my trip was winding down as well. Fall was fast approaching; school buses were back on the road, aspen were changing and dry fly-fishing had slowed, at least temporarily, at least enough for me to be able to turn my back on it and make my getaway. If

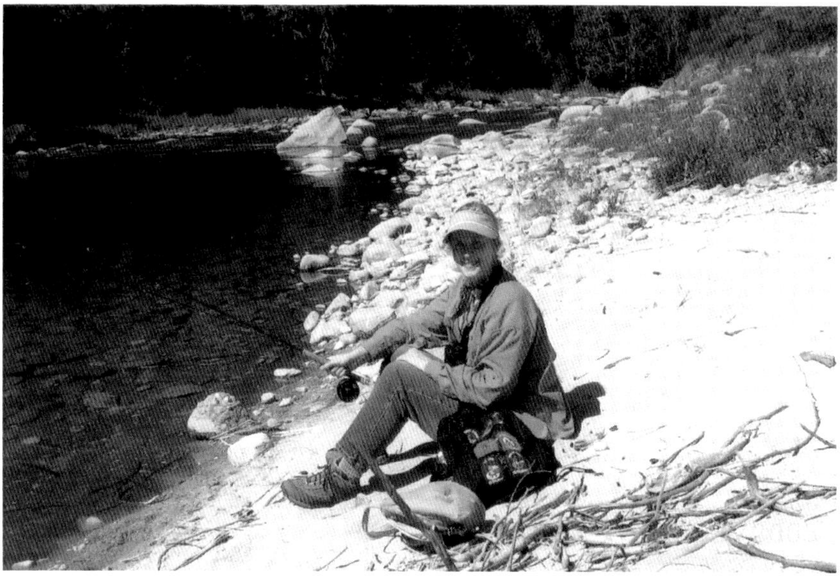

Patricia Dickson beside the Lochsa River, Montana.

that Trico hatch had lasted indefinitely, I don't know what I would have done. And for others, I'm sure the salmon fly hatch would have the same effect, or the Mother's Day caddis. Those of us who, in the presence of rising fish, lack self-control—probably most fly fishermen—are fortunate that these hatches are seasonal and self-limited.

I gradually fished my way out of state, west to east. To cleanse my palate of the bitter taste of paying too much for a room in Big Sky, I spent the last night camped on the upper Stillwater. The night was cold and clear and stars were almost too brilliant, too imposing, more like frothy champagne bubbles than like the Milky Way. Proust would have blown a gasket.

In the morning, I made a few perfunctory casts and a leisurely departure. What was the rush? It would be another week before fall fishing in Maine was ripe. And then, with luck and the right weather, it would last another eight weeks.

For once I was ready to return to Maine, and I could already tell that the Maine to which I was returning differed from the Maine I'd left. Too much of my earlier Maine fishing was spoiled by a distracted mind that not even good fishing could relieve. Those were days when I fretted over not living elsewhere, out west perhaps. But time and distance had purged those days of their impurities, and I could see them now for what they were and for what, except for my imperfect vision, they always had been: absolutely wonderful days on the water. And time had also taught me that, vital as the act and circumstances of fly-fishing were to my happiness, size and numbers of fish were not.

Those Maine waters that I had not allowed myself to fully appreciate at the time could now rise and take their rightful places among the more highly celebrated Western rivers. It was, in a sense, *time regained*, but more importantly it was fish and waters regained: the Cupsuptic, Cold Stream, Kennebago, Spencer Stream, North Branch of the Dead, the Kennebec, thc East Outlet, Kibby Stream, Parker Pond and Torsey Pond, bass, trout and salmon and the lush greenery of Maine—compared to the arid West—the fiddleheads, the dense mixed forests and moss-covered boulders. Places that I had not let touch me now could and did. It all made me appreciate how lucky I was to live in such a wonderful place, to live anywhere with cold flowing water. I could hardly wait to get back home and go fishing.

The Maiden Voyage of the *Little Pat*

Four of us were having dinner, Dan, his wife Pat, my girlfriend (also Pat) and I. That week Dan and I had just taken my twelve-foot aluminum boat out of mothballs and were looking for a place for her inaugural voyage. Dan had bought a six-horse engine, pair of oars and fresh set of numbers. We hadn't discussed a name. "We're calling her the *Little Pat*," I said.

The women laughed. At least we were attempting to make them feel a part of the conversation. Then Dan and I tried to decide where to fish. Dan suggested Houston Brook Pond, but I vetoed that. "That's one you'll have to do alone," I said. "Too much work for a few tiny brookies." It's a beautiful place, steep valley with a naturally dammed brook, but there's a short cliff you have to slither down and then clamber back up. With a boat?

"Where then?" asked Dan.

"What about the Andro?"

"I'm not fishing for those cross-eyed fish."

That was an allusion to the Androscoggin's past history as one of the most polluted rivers in America. Now the upper river was relatively clean and held some nice trout, none of which had crossed eyes. But this was not the time to argue. The good feeling generated by the *Little Pat* remark had dissipated. The ladies were visibly restless and bored. "We'll talk about this later," I said.

Afterward, my Pat, who had never met Dan before, said, "It doesn't sound like this fishing trip is going to work out."

I laughed. "Oh, it'll work out. We'll go somewhere," I said. "We've been doing this for years. It's like jury selection. I toss out one of his choices. He tosses out one of mine. But eventually we'll settle on something."

Which was exactly what happened. Later, over the phone, Dan and I agreed on the East Outlet of the Kennebec. We'd launch the *Little Pat* at Indian Pond and motor up to the inlet. We both like fishing the East Outlet. An excellent compromise.

However, two days before our trip, I'd had a good midweek outing on the Andro. I caught several nice rainbows covering rises with tiny dries. "It was *great* fun," I said. "Those fish really fight."

This was Saturday morning and we were in Dan's new truck, already en route to the East Outlet. The *Little Pat* fit perfectly into the truck bed, as if the truck and boat were made for each other. Dan slowed.

"Maybe we ought to forget about going to the East Outlet and just fish the Andro," he said.

"I thought you didn't want to fish for 'cross-eyed fish.'" I knew he'd only said that because I'd insulted Houston Brook Pond. If you insult a fisherman's favorite water, you insult him.

"Well, the Androscoggin is a lot closer than the East Outlet."

"Keep in mind, I was fishing midweek. I had no competition. Who knows what the weekend will be like?"

"Sounds like you're getting nervous now that I called your bluff."

"I'm always willing to fish the Andro. I just don't want to compromise your principles."

He looked at his watch. It was already half past seven. The older we got, the later we started. We were approaching Farmington Falls: right would take us to the East Outlet, left to the Andro. "Your call," I said. He turned left.

We already had a plan; we'd had one since the first time we fished the Andro two falls ago. We'd put the boat in at the takeout and motor to a huge pool about half a mile *up*river, a pool that the fishermen drifting down—the usual approach—would not reach until late in the day, after we had already pounded it. Countercurrent fishing, contrarian fishing. Of course, there were a lot of unknowns, such as, would the boat float? Would the engine start? Was there enough water to motor upriver? What about rocks, logs and other obstacles?

The boat floated, the engine started and, kneeling in the bow, I directed Dan around submerged rocks and gravel bars. When we reached the tail of our target pool, fish were rising, big fish. The air was calm, speckled with insects—mayflies, caddis and stones. While Dan was rigging up, I stumbled across the shingle and waded toward the lowermost of the three fish rising in the center cut.

I tied on a small caddis and waded out as far as safely possible. A heavy slab of current separated me from the fish. I worked out line and made a few casts, but could barely reach the fish and couldn't avoid drag. I tried several other dries, then a nymph with strike indicator, but still no luck.

Dan went above me to where other fish were rising and immediately hooked up. "Damn chub!" he said. The Andro is full of chub, trophy chub that mix in with the trout.

"I don't think these are chub," I said. You can never be sure, but these fish were moving too much water; the rises made significant dents, and sometimes you could see backs and tails. Also, chub don't make my hands shake.

I *wanted* one of these fish, and by then I didn't care how I got it. I had something to prove. As a last resort I tied on a Gray Ghost, my ultimate trout weapon. If the fly was going to drag, make it look intentional. Swim the streamer; let it swoop down past fish. I did, and when I tightened up on my very first full cast, I felt a heavy take. "Fish on!" I yelled. Dan turned just in time to see the fish jump. "That is not a chub," he said.

"No, it's a nice rainbow," I said.

I was wrong; it was a nice brown, a measured sixteen inches, thick and dark. I was happy and relieved. It took a while to land the fish in the heavy current, but amazingly the fish had not disturbed the others, which were still rising above me. I waded carefully up a few yards and made another long cast with my streamer, let it swing, tightened up and felt another heavy take, but no jump. "This is a better fish," I said.

In the strong current, this fish would not be easily subdued. I was in no hurry. Dan moved down next to me for a better look and to help. This was good, except that his net was tiny. "You need a bigger net," I said. "These aren't brookies."

But he wanted to try and I wanted him to see this fish close up, to feel its weight. "That's a *big* fish," Dan said as the trout swung close by, then swirled and took more line. At that point, I didn't care if he netted him or knocked him loose. He had seen the fish and shown respect.

Somehow Dan managed to fold that brown into his twelve-inch trout net; it didn't hurt the fish—they bend—and it helped us. He hefted him, net and all. "That's a heavy fish," he said.

I unhooked the brown, measured him at seventeen inches and held him by the tail in the current until he pulled free. "So what do you think of the Andro now?" I asked.

"I'm impressed."

That was all it took to bring us back into synch. We were on the same page now, the same team. And we were just getting started.

This pool is several hundred yards long and bends to our upriver left against a sandbank perhaps fifty feet high. The current is imperceptible until you attempt to wade or cast. In the morning calm, the pool's surface was unmarred, mirroring the sky, except in the pond-like belly of the pool, where rising fish pockmarked the glassy surface. We motored up, anchored to the side of the main current and waited for the fish we'd put down to resume rising. We did not have to wait long. Dan covered the rises with a small dark caddis and immediately began catching rainbows from fourteen to sixteen inches. Some jumped, some didn't, but in the heavy current none came easily to the net. Dan was ecstatic. After he'd caught a few, he turned to me. "Your turn to fish," he said.

I shook my head. "This is your punishment for insulting this river. You have to fish until your arm falls off."

When these fish stopped rising, he switched to a streamer and caught more. Then other fish began rising at the head of the pool, slashing like bluefish. By the time we'd repositioned the boat, the fish had stopped rising. Rather than wait, Dan cast a streamer and immediately hooked a bright rainbow. On his next five casts he hooked fish, all rainbows, fourteen to sixteen inches.

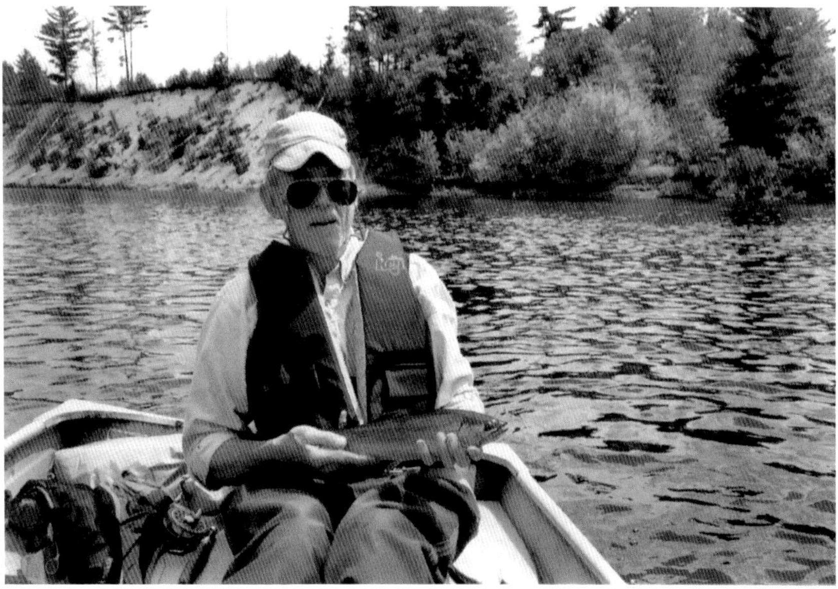

Dan in the *Little Pat* with an Androscoggin River rainbow.

By then it was afternoon. We dropped downriver to the next pool, one we'd motored through but hadn't fished. More rising rainbows. We both fished now, sometimes wading, sometimes casting from the boat. And the pool below that one produced more fish still. We fished all day and were never long away from trout. The weather stayed mild, with a milky sky, a mellow breeze and miraculously few biting insects, but plenty of caddis and mayflies. It was easily the best day I'd ever had on that river, one of the best days either of us had had anywhere, a rare day when the elements, the gear and fish all worked to perfection. And the pleasure was doubled by Dan's presence and doubled again by his earlier insult.

Dan had fished here before, but at the takeout he looked at the river as if seeing it for the first time. "It's like a big Western river," he said, surveying the surrounding mountains, the braided runs and gravel bars. "It's like the Missouri."

Comparing Maine water, *any* water, to a Montana river is the ultimate compliment. It's like saying your girlfriend has "movie star" good looks. All was forgiven.

While Dan went to retrieve the truck, I held the boat in a gentle side chute. I was very proud of that river. How many times do we brag about a pond or river, then take somebody and have the water not perform? But not this time. This time the river came through. It outdid itself. "You big showoff," I said, running my fingers through the current.

Addendum: That was 2003, and since then something happened to that river. The fishing just isn't the same on that section of the Androscoggin. Otherwise I wouldn't have called the river by its real name. On the other hand, this river has been down before and, with help, which it is receiving, it will likely be back again. A river has as many lives as we give it.

Dan from Fritz to Sam

I've known Dan Onion since his son Fritz was three years old, hunkered between us in Dan's canoe as we hunted ducks on the Lummi Indian Reservation near Bellingham, Washington. And Dan has known my son Preston since Preston was in utero. In fact, Dan's the one who found him there, a little nubbin so small and unobtrusive that Preston's parents had not even noticed.

The duck hunts were in 1970, when Dan and I were medical residents in Seattle. In '72 we both moved back East and by '75 were both living in Maine. Dan had taken the direct route. I had taken a route so circuitous—involving one year of hunting and fishing and two years of doctoring in Virginia—that Dan didn't even know I was in Maine until my wife took ill, and I needed his help.

After a confused phone conversation—"No, not Mount Vernon, Washington. Mount Vernon, Maine!"—Dan agreed to see her in his Farmington clinic, a mere twenty minutes away. While Dan examined my wife, I sat in the small waiting room, reading an outdoor magazine. Soon Dan came to speak with me. He had a funny look on his face.

"Jim, she's late," he said. "And she's having morning sickness."

"Yeah, and epigastric pain and hematemasis," I countered. To me it seemed a pretty straightforward case of gastritis, or maybe an ulcer. She'd been under a lot of stress—a recent move, a new job and me.

"'When you hear hoofbeats…'"

"Dan, please, don't patronize me with clichés, okay? I went to medical school too." I hated that hackneyed saying, "When you hear hoofbeats, think of horses, not zebras." Did he think I didn't know that?

"Well, we'll check it out just in case."

"Fine. Suit yourself."

I should have known better than to argue medicine with Dan. When he was in medical training he carried on his belt, in a pair of cardboard, homemade "holsters," index cards of medical references and abstracts of journal articles. On ward rounds, in the middle of a heated debate on a complex case, Dan would whip out a card, cite chapter and verse—"*New England Journal*, August '64…38 percent of patients…"—and settle the issue. He was teased mercilessly for those holsters and references—*nobody* did this—but he didn't care, and one day that ridiculous collection of index cards became *The Little Black Book of Primary Care*, now in its fourth—or is it fifth?—edition, and exploded into a series of related books all edited by Dan. As I said, I should have known better than to argue medicine with him.

And so, of course, that straightforward case of gastritis turned out to be Preston, my first nonfishing son.

Dan went on to have two daughters, Amanda and Alene, in addition to Fritz, and I had another son, Evan. They're all nice people, smart and accomplished. Fritz has also written books, quite successful books about computers and programming. But for all their talents and accomplishments, not one of those five children is a fisherman. Yes, occasionally one or another of the five would accompany Dan or me fishing, and we have the pictures to prove it. I have one of Preston, age three, holding a pickerel on a forked stick. That would've been on an Atlantic salmon trip—because who takes pickerel trips?—to the Denny's River in Downeast Maine that our families made together in 1979.

Fritz used to fish the Kennebago with Dan and, cruelly, caught the largest landlocked salmon any of us had taken from that river. Alene still goes with her dad on the lower Kennebec, and a few summers ago my son Evan took two nice bass from Morse Pond, but it was his first fishing trip with me since he was old enough to say "No," and he hasn't gone since.

Now our children are all grown up. A few years ago Fritz married Susan, and they begat Zoe and Samuel. Zoe is a striking redhead, bright, theatrical and articulate, but she does not fish. Sam, however, is a different story.

In 2002 Sam, age four, freckled and cute as a Norman Rockwell painting, was visiting Dan's lakeside home in central Maine. A small tributary of Flying Pond runs along Dan's property line. Sam sat on a boulder beside the stream, staring into the flowing water for many long minutes. From a distance Dan watched Sam watch the stream, because

Dan realized his grandson was not gazing idly at the water, daydreaming. Dan knew the signs: that child was *studying* the water. Finally Sam slid off the boulder and came running over. "Grandpa," he said excitedly, "I think that stream holds *fish*!"

Sam's excitement could not have exceeded Dan's as he told me this story. "I think he's got the fishing gene," Dan said.

"Sure sounds like it," I said, enviously.

In 2003, Dan bought Sam a fly-fishing outfit, and on a cold April morning they stopped by the house after fishing. The ice was not even gone from Lovejoy Pond; I hadn't even bought a fishing license yet, but Dan had found some open water, to which he had taken Sam and his new fly rod. They had not caught a thing. "Too early, I guess," Dan said unnecessarily. We were standing beside his truck in the chilly, paltry April sun.

"I would think so," I said, shivering and giving Dan a skeptical look.

This sort of premature fishing exposure can ruin some kids, or at least set them back, but not Sam. He didn't whine or complain about having been dragged out in the cold for no fish. He wore a stocking cap and a winter jacket, and his small fingers were red from the cold, but he did not seem the least discouraged. "You want to show Jim your new fly rod?" Dan asked.

Sam nodded, and they gently removed the rod from the truck bed. Sam held it out proudly for me to see.

"Nice outfit," I said.

He smiled shyly. His freckles are so neat and circular, they seem almost painted on, like makeup, and his blue eyes were bright and full of hope. Some five-year-olds might already have made the connection between fly rod, cold fingers and sleep loss, but not Sam. Instead he seemed to sense the rod's potential, the future happiness that it, like a magic wand, might provide. "Your grandfather is a very lucky man," I said.

The next time I saw Dan he had another Sam fishing story. When warm weather finally arrived, Sam had returned to his grandparents' and he and Dan had fished from the dock on Flying Pond. This time Sam was using worms for sunfish. "He talks to the fish, Jim! He tells them how to bite. It works too!" Sam caught sunfish after sunfish. He was indefatigable. Fly-casting beside him, Dan hooked a large bass on a Wooly Bugger. He handed the rod to Sam, but the bass pulled too hard. "I can't reel him," Sam said. And when the fish jumped, it startled Sam. It was "scary." So he handed the rod back to his grandfather, who proceeded to land the bass, a smallmouth. By then Sam was once again preoccupied with the sunfish; he had resumed the conversation that Dan had interrupted. And that is how it starts, this obsessive relationship between man and fish, or boy and fish, with a conversation, a dialogue. Only a nonfisherman would call it a monologue.

Sam at Grant's Camps

The Kennebago River, northwest of Rangeley, Maine, was discovered on a blazing hot July afternoon in 1975 by J.H. Hall. At least it felt like a discovery.

In those pre–Delorme Atlas days, relying on an outdated geologic survey map and a compass, I probed several spurs off Lincoln Pond Road before locating one that led within earshot of the river. There was no trail; I broke brush, climbed over dry-kill and around boulders, ascended a final ridge, slid down a gravel bank and then finally saw the river glistening in sunlight—the Kennebago, meaning "Land of Sweetly Flowing Waters." Even the name was beautiful.

Directly across from me was a small, curved, tantalizing pool. Imagine the fishing in so remote a spot! It was at that moment that a brown station wagon bearing Massachusetts license tags pulled up across the river, within feet of the pool, and four men in waders tumbled out and began assembling their gear.

"Sons of bitches," I said, not realizing that a decade later Dan and I would be those very sons of bitches. "Where did they come from?"

They came from Grant's Kennebago Camps, a venerable set of sporting camps on Kennebago Lake. I'd heard of them but, unemployed at the time, I was not prepared to pay to fish a river that was accessible to anyone willing to do the work required to circumvent the gate, which barred access to the nine miles of road—the abandoned rail bed—that paralleled the river. It's a common arrangement in Maine between the public and the large paper companies that own the land (a truce currently endangered by the paper companies reinventing themselves as real estate barons).

For the next decade I waged a guerilla fishing war against the patrons of Grant's Camps—"Grantees" I dubbed them, because, in any conflict, in order to keep your edge, you need to stereotype the enemy. Orvis-clad, Volvo-driving yuppies were the stereotype. Every so often, though, due to poor planning, I would meet my fishing competition on the river and, surprisingly, they seemed like very decent people. But I could never forget that they had bought their ways past that gate, whereas I had biked and hiked. I never beat them to the famous upriver pools such as Cedar, Powerhouse, Lunch, Canoe and certainly not John's, but I found excellent, neglected water downriver, but above the gate, and I caught my share of fish.

In those days, Dan was too busy practicing medicine, logging his land, raising a family and tending to farm animals, including oxen (which he pulled in the Franklin County Fair, possibly the only physician ever to do so)—too busy, in other words, to fish much. But in the early 1980s, he finally got his priorities straight, sold one ox, butchered and ate the other (quite tasty) and began fishing the Kennebago with me, guerilla style, biking and hiking.

Dan had a friend, Clint, who owned a small camp on Kennebago Lake, and in September of 1985 he offered it for a weekend. We accepted. It

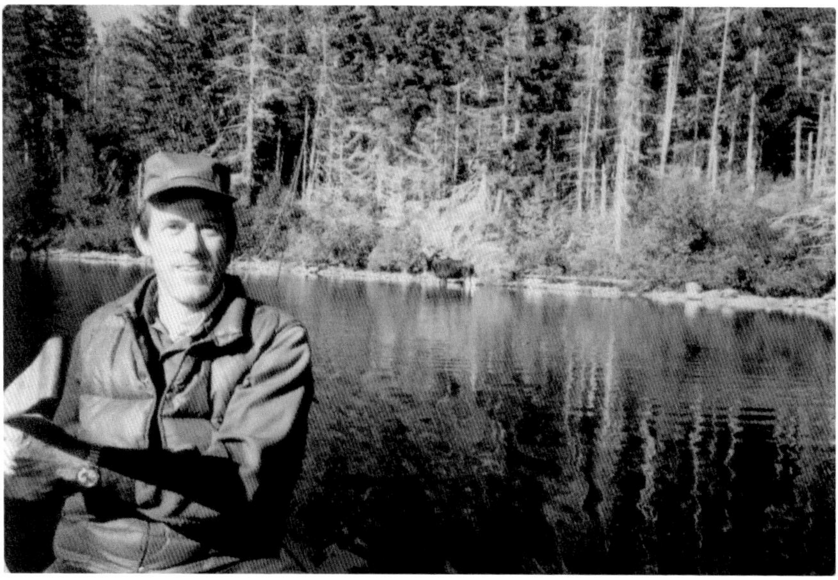

Dan on Kennebago Lake, circa 1985. Note the bull moose in the background.

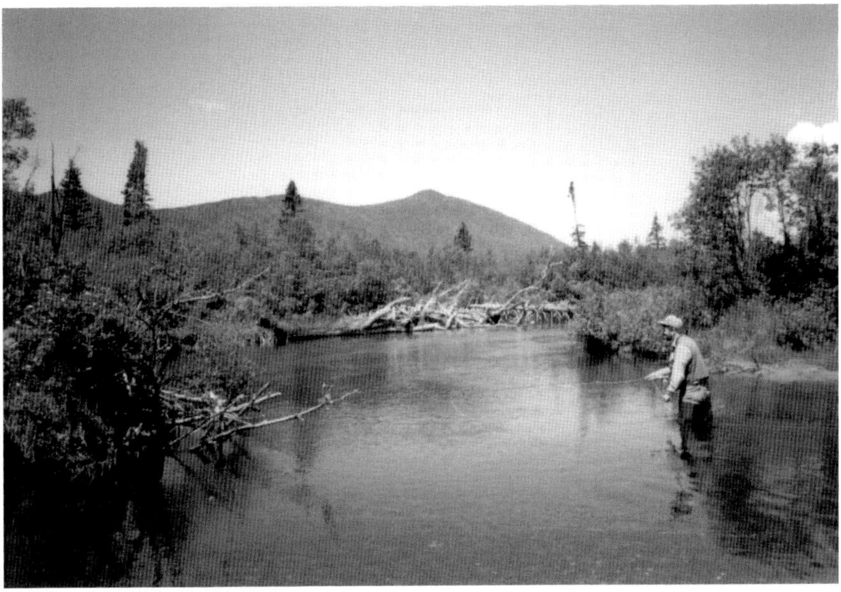

The author on the upper Kennebago River.

was a strange sensation to arrive at the river, not short of breath, without leg cramps and with fingers unbitten by frost from the long bike ride up the logging road on a chilly morning. "This is almost too easy, isn't it?" I said.

"Almost," said Dan, "but not quite." His commitment to my guerilla fishing tactics left something to be desired.

We fished the river for parts of three days and did well. The fish did not seem to care how we arrived. A Gray Ghost was a Gray Ghost. As we were packing to leave, Dan said, "I'd like to check out Grant's before we go."

"I'd just as soon not stay there," I said. I had a part-time job by then; money wasn't the issue. Hard to say exactly what the issue was.

"Won't hurt to look," he said.

We looked, and there was no escaping the fact that Grant's Camps were beautiful: classic log cabins with green roofs, on the south shore of Kennebago Lake, looking across the dappled waters to Cow Ridge, Snow Mountain and, down the lake, to West Kennebago, already in fall colors, a scarlet swath of deciduous trees below the darker spruce and fir.

Even the price was reasonable: fifty-five dollars a night per person, all meals included. And the lady at the front desk was cordial, if not encouraging. "What time of year were you looking for?" she asked.

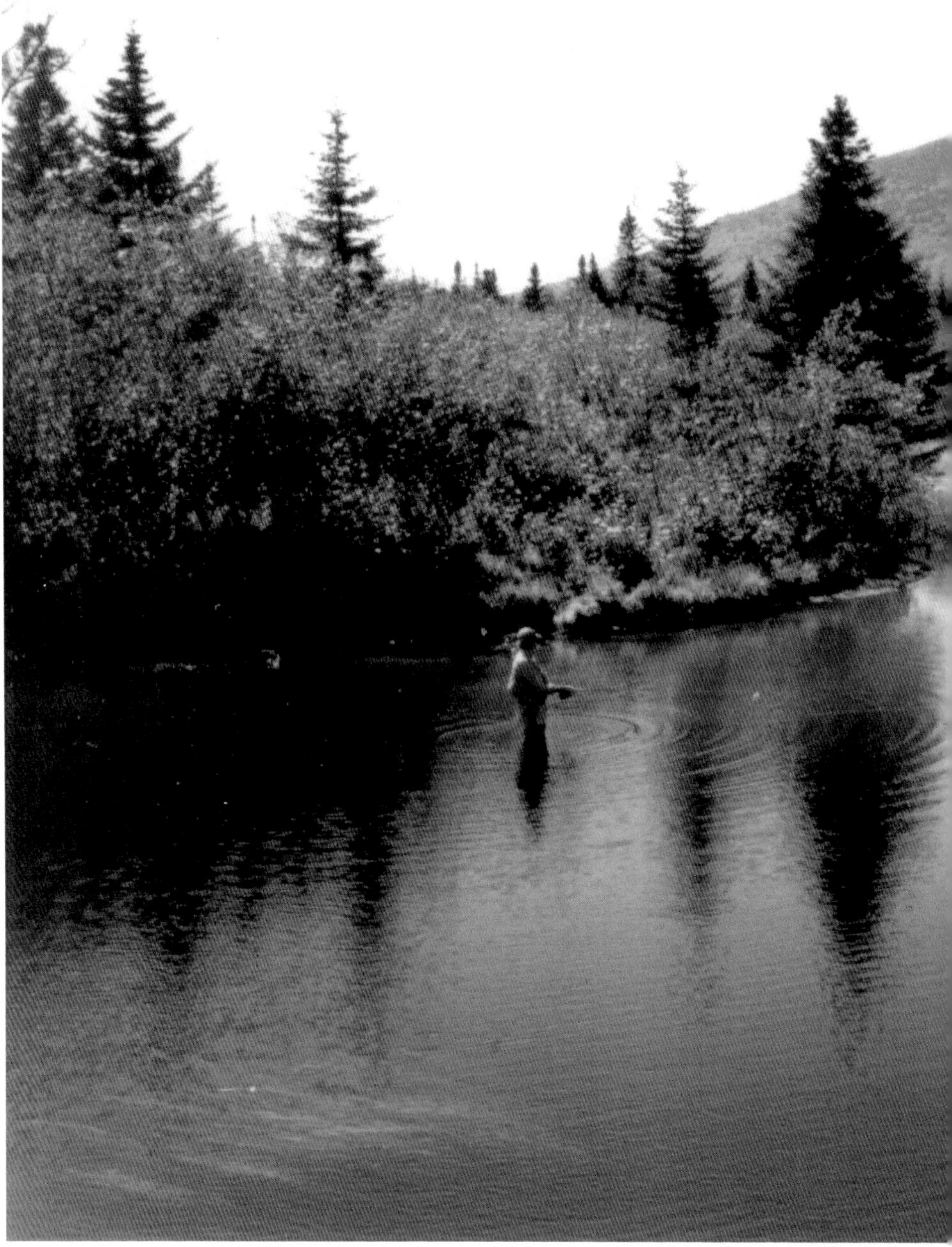

Dan on the upper Kennebago River.

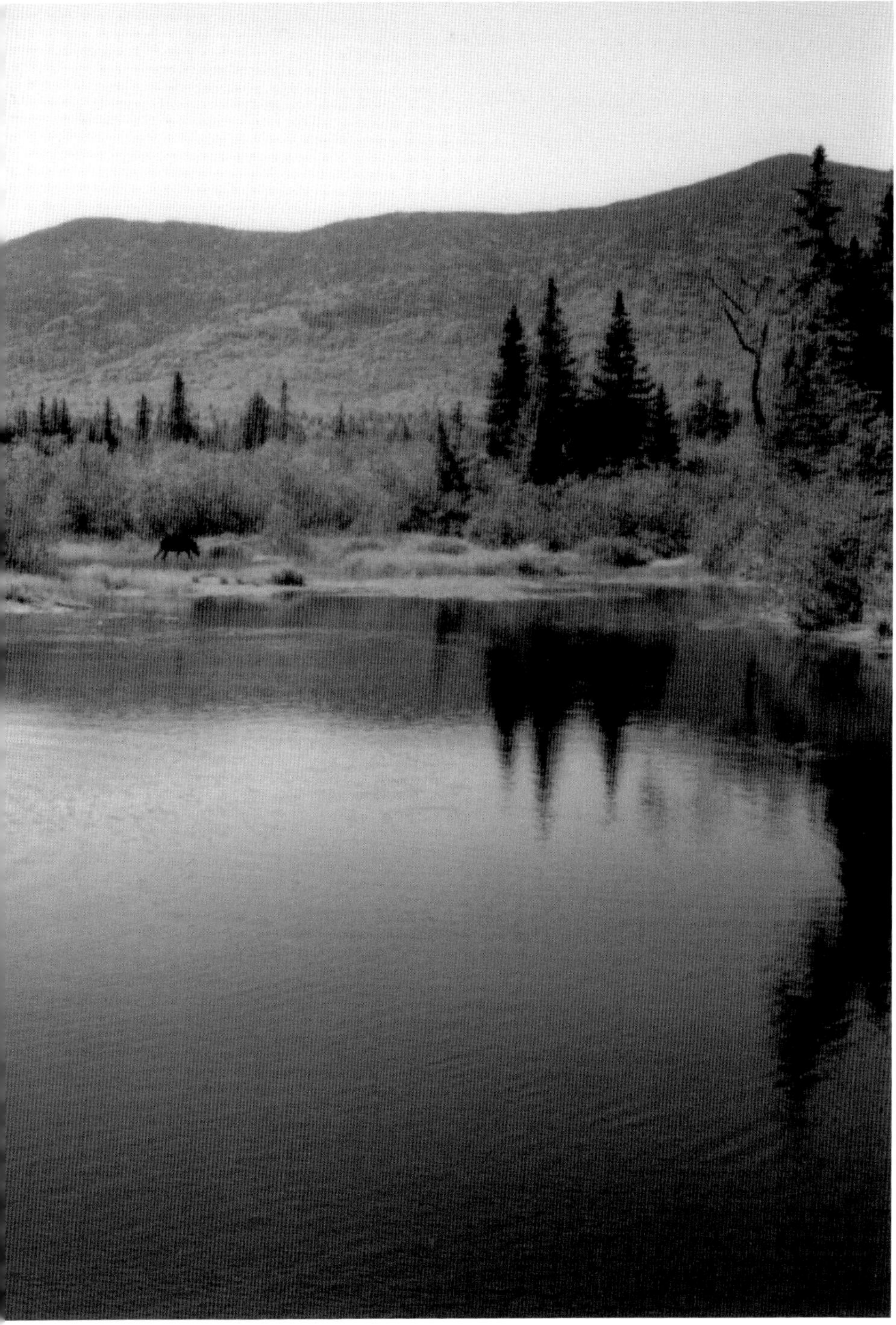

"About this time, next year," said Dan.

The lady made a sad face and flipped through a few pages of her reservation book. "September and June are our busiest times," she said. "We're booked years in advance with return customers. I can put you on the waiting list. We do get cancellations."

"Okay."

She added our names to the bottom of the list, which was already a dozen names long. I was indifferent, but Dan walked out despondent.

Before we'd gotten ten feet outside the office, we ran into Walter (Skeet) Davenport, longtime Maine guide, manager and part owner of Grant's and, more to the point, a former patient of Dan's.

Skeet greeted him like an old friend. "You planning on staying with us, Doc?"

"Well, we wanted to. We couldn't get in. You're all booked."

Skeet seemed undaunted. "When was it you wanted to stay?"

"We were hoping to get this date next year; we did pretty well the last few days."

"You just wait right here a minute," Skeet said. "Let me see what I can do. There's two of you, right?"

We waited, and in a very few minutes Skeet came out to tell us we were booked for next September, three nights. We even got a couple of dates in June.

"You must have done one hell of a job on his leg," I said later.

One visit was enough to win me over, and since then, we've become regulars at Grant's. We've been through two—or is it three?—sets of owners; we've seen the prices rise and the fishing, at least in the river, decline. But through it all, Grant's has retained its same charm, evocative of a bygone era. The dining hall resembles a museum of mounted fish, historic photos and artwork by guests. The food is plentiful, the staff unfailingly gracious and the view as beautiful and placid as ever. Waterfowl still feed in the shallows, moose still stroll the shoreline and loons still serenade one's sleep with their melancholy ululations—actually they make a racket, but many people apparently enjoy it. Adding to the tranquility is a total absence of jet skis and high-powered outboards. The camp's classic Rangeley boats, with their green lapstrake sides, graceful lines and small, quiet engines, simply add to the atmosphere.

This June 2007, Sam came along. Actually it was I who "came along." It was Sam and Dan's trip. Sam had come the previous June, but evidently they'd missed the hatch and Sam's attention had lagged. "He got a little bored," Dan said, as if the child had contracted an illness. "Your job is to keep up his enthusiasm."

"Right," I said. My job, as always, would be to catch fish. If that kept Sam's enthusiasm up, so much the better. Perhaps he'd benefit from watching a seasoned angler in action; perhaps he'd learn a thing or two.

I joined them in the middle of a hot June day. That morning Dan and Sam had had no luck on the lake; I'd sampled two downriver pools on my way in and caught little. We ate lunch; we lazed around. In fact, I don't recall exactly what we did because there were no fish involved.

Evening found us anchored beyond the causeway in a shallow weedy section, known as "the Logans." As the sun moved behind West Kennebago Mountain, the temperature fell and our spirits and expectations rose. A few trout dimpled the surface. Dan assisted Sam in the stern; I cast from the bow. Soon Sam began hooking small trout, and some that were not so small, twelve inches or more, not lunkers by any means, but fish that could not, or should not, be simply snatched in. They required finesse, and Sam, as Dan proudly pointed out, had learned how to play fish, when and how to give line and when to take it. He was doing well. I was having difficulty. Nothing I tried, not a Royal Wulff, Adams, Light Cahill, Red Quill, Dark Cahill or caddis worked. The only fly that worked was a Hornberg, specifically Sam's Hornberg, which he had taken to calling a "Fishburger," I suppose because the fish took to it so ravenously. The whole evening he never changed that fly. He took fish after fish on the fly until it was falling apart and didn't resemble a Hornberg anymore, or even a fly. Yet it still worked, whereas nothing I tried—I had no Hornbergs—did. I made some fanciful excuses, which seemed to amuse Sam, but soon he pushed me one fish over the line, and I said, "For crying out loud, Sam, what are you doing?"

"You gotta move the fly, Jim. And you gotta use a 'Fishburger.'"

"Did I just ask a nine-year-old for fishing advice?"

"Sounded like it," Dan said.

The thing was, it was good advice, and Dan gave me a Hornberg, aka "Fishburger," and by moving it, as Sam advised, I actually hooked a fish, in the tail. "Takes talent to hook 'em in the tail," I said. "Anybody can catch 'em in the mouth. They got teeth up there."

Then, as if to prove my point, I hooked one in the mouth and promptly snapped him off. Sam laughed.

The rest of the evening was a blur of laughter and brook trout—Sam's brook trout—and banter that, because we were high on fish,

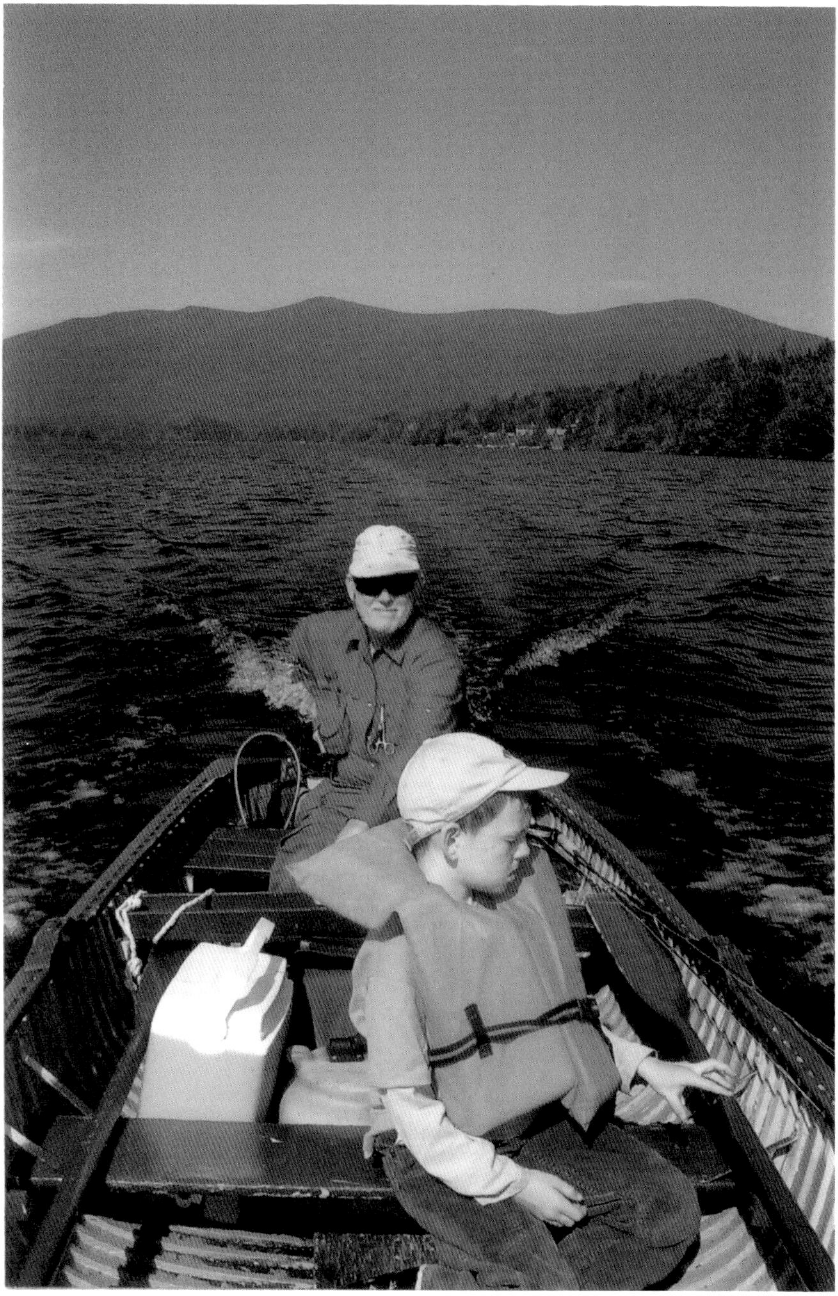

Dan and Sam on Kennebago Lake, 2007.

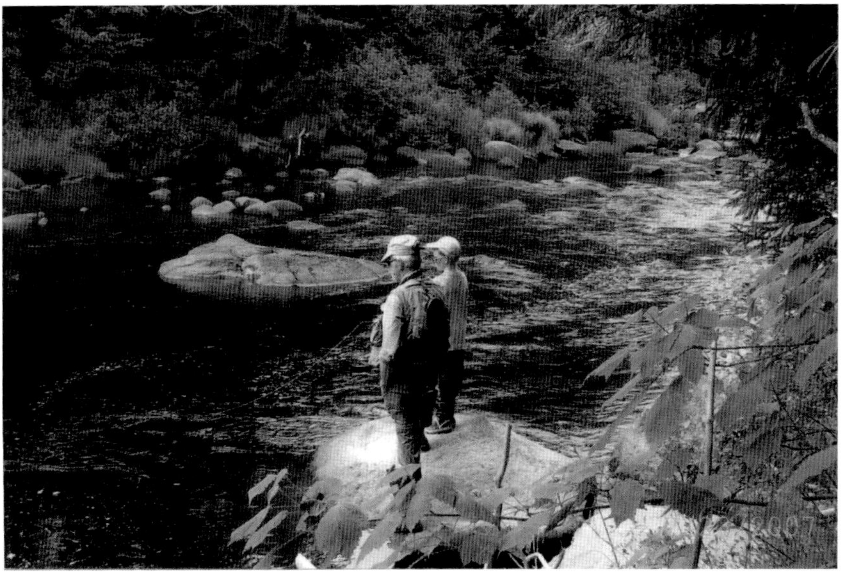

Dan and Sam on the lower Kennebago River.

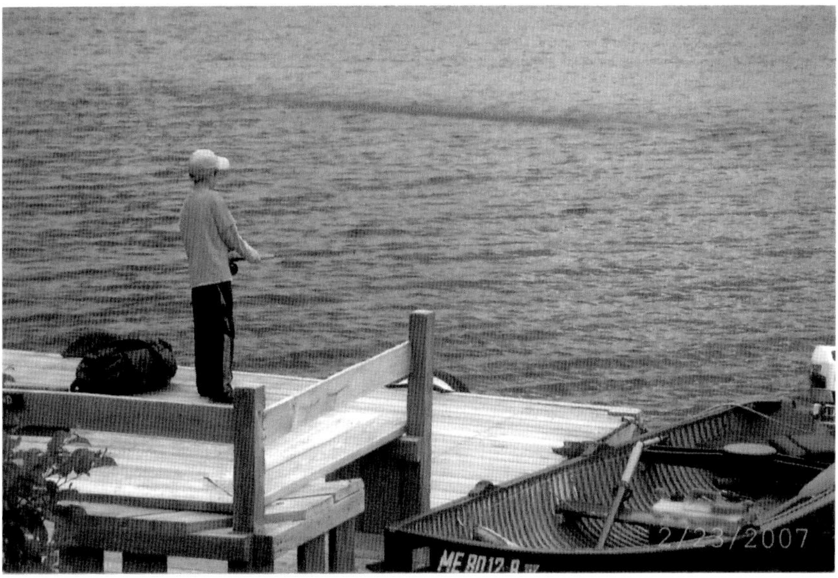

Sam enjoys a quiet moment alone on Kennebago Lake.

seemed hilarious at the time. As if that weren't enough, a loon was stalking us, lurking like a mugger until someone—okay, Sam—hooked a trout. Then the loon would dive in like a submarine in pursuit of the desperate fish. The loon swam directly under the boat, its sinister black beak and tapered body easily visible even in the fading light. (And they warn *us* not to harass loons?)

And still Sam caught fish, and still with the same "Fishburger," to which he had become as attached as to a stuffed animal or hamster. It took on human characteristics; it had personality. It was cute, and fish loved it.

Later Dan tried to give me credit for keeping Sam amused, but this was demonstrably untrue: that very afternoon the same three of us had been listless and bored, without hope—until the fish appeared. That was when Sam became enthused and Jim became "amusing." It is part of the fish's catalytic magic: they make grown men giggle, embolden nine-year-olds to give advice and allow older men to take it. And small fish create disproportionately large memories, indelible memories, in which they, the trout, modestly step aside to make room for the memories' real stars. I'd be willing to bet that long after Sam has forgotten the trout he caught, maybe even after he's forgotten the "Fishburger," he will remember being in the stern of that skiff at sunset with his grandfather, laughing and laughing, even if he can't quite remember why.